From Defeat to Victory

A Soldier's Story

T.M. Faunce

xulon PRESS

Copyright © 2015 by T.M. Faunce

From Defeat To Victory
(A Soldier's Story)
by T.M. Faunce

Printed in the United States of America

ISBN 9781498423663

All rights reserved solely by the author. The author guarantees all contents are original and do not infringe upon the legal rights of any other person or work. No part of this book may be reproduced in any form without the permission of the author. The views expressed in this book are not necessarily those of the publisher.

Unless otherwise indicated, Scripture quotations are taken from the King James Version (KJV) – public domain.

Cover Art Work by: T. M. Faunce

www.xulonpress.com

"A Soldier's Story"
(From defeat, to victory)

Introduction

Often we hear someone say, "He or she is a self made person". A serious person realizes, when someone makes such statements either of himself or others that no one is self made! All of us, to a certain extent are partially the product of other persons and/or of culture. By resolve and commitment we may escape culture. Those persons we know and with whom we associate may become part of us as "examples". Most successful persons on inquiry admit to having been influenced by persons chosen as "examples".

God crossed my path with several such persons whom I found to be unusual and whom I believe worthy of "example". Of course I know by faith and the Word that life's ultimate and eternal "example" is Lord Jesus Christ, obedient Son of God, "not only an example, but the Way!"

My maternal Grandmother became my "example" for love and compassion. As a young grandson I saw in her life "patience" and "long suffering" for me and others. She is an "example" which I have done my best to follow. At age twelve, there came into my life a very old man. He was my Sunday school teacher. His life reached back to our civil war period, early 1860's. Mr. Rushton was his name and his commitment to our Lord's "service" was worthy and lasting "example". I loved Mr. Rushton and have never forgotten him. Later during a teenage crisis, a professor in my high school became my "example" for "encouragement". Tony Markert was his name and I warmly recall him till this very day. There are others.

This book, by Thomas M. Faunce, begins sadly and in defeat, however its end brings Glory to His Father while becoming an "example" of Great "Faith" for me. Yes, in each occasion described in "A SOLDIER'S STORY", Tom demonstrates by worthy "example", great "faith", "determination" and "courage. I first met Tom about 1995 during a Christian mission trip to South India. During that trip, I observed the man committed to Lord Jesus Christ as well as a serious and equipped Evangelist.

Since that mission trip, I have participated with and observed him as he, with intense commitment, visited Southeastern Europe (Bosnia), Central America and Mexico, Sudan, South Asia, after Tsunami, and other areas devastated by war or natural disaster. Tom often gathers medical and other supplies for people whom he has never seen or known, and by great "faith" and resolve traveled to those war torn areas not expecting anyone to meet him and not knowing whether the local government would confiscate the well hidden Bibles and other supplies or even permit him to enter the country or area. God always worked those matters out, honoring Tom's great "faith".

He always takes along the "Jesus Film" with the correct language (or dialect), plus projector, generator, etc. Most times many persons experience their "new birth" and/or grow as "disciples", when Tom tells about his Savior, Lord Jesus Christ.

My human example for "faith" is Tom's "faith". He is attracted to human disasters and on each occasion has prepared for his travels with commitment and perfect resolve. Tom's love for his fellow man and humility are obvious. I praise God that He permitted my life's path to come along side Tom's in this our "pilgrimage", called "life".

This writer has participated in over 30 short term World Wide Christian ministries on most continents and is familiar with the numerous requirements and problems in making such ministries happen.

Therefore, "FROM DEFEAT TO VICTORY" is a book strongly recommended by this friend of Thomas M. Faunce, Founder and Director of Frontline Outreach Ministries.

Harry Jeffcoat, Jr.
Birmingham, Alabama

Forward

I think the greatest compliment a man can receive is that "he lives what he preaches". I can say this without reservation about Tom Faunce. Any man that this statement can be said about him needs to write his life story. We have to know the journey that God brought him on to get to this point.

There are some that have incredible testimonies and never do anything with their lives. They live off a past story, never creating new testimonies with their transformed life. Not in this book. "FROM DEFEAT TO VICTORY" is about the kingdom of God taking over a man's life, and how he can be used to advance our Saviour's rule, regardless of where you come from or where that nation is. Tom's story should give every praying parent hope that our Jesus is God of the impossible.

The grace of God that brought Tom from the miry clay has also brought him around the world to preach the Gospel. That's what makes this book special. He not only has a testimony but he is watching God, through Frontline Outreach, create testimonies around the world. Regardless of the political upheaval of that nation the economic poverty, military (cods) or famine, Tom and Frontline are on the frontlines preaching the message of the kingdom.

I have been preaching and pastoring for over 21 years. And when I need to have my life challenged, realize the vanity of things of this world, and have spirit ignited for world missions, I meet with Tom Faunce. His life makes me want to be more like Jesus. Don't read this like a normal testimony or biography or you will miss the message. Tom is a preacher, a missionary, a prophet and a spokesperson to every believer who find themselves being lured by the legitimate things of this world, and in the process lose a zeal for the things we should be passionate about.

The life and life story of Tom Faunce makes the words of Francis of Assisi come alive………..

- "Preach the gospel to everyone, and whenever needful use words."
- Pastor Tim Dilena Revival Tabernacle Highland Park Mich.

From Defeat to Victory
Chapter 1

It was February 2, 1968, when I exited the plane. The heat of the South East Asia night was like a furnace. I was barely eighteen, with no idea of what awaited me in this strange and faraway land. A sergeant was shouting at us to hurry off the plane. We were the new troops and we had landed right in the middle of what was called the Tet offense. Flares lit up the night sky, while helicopters overhead fired mini guns. Waves of tracers filled the air, glowing red like fire. Off in the distance, mortar rounds were exploding and the burst of machine gun fire shattered the night's silence. We all ran toward a quonset hut, my head lowered and my heart filled with anxious thoughts of home. As we entered the building, other young men were being hurried out to the plane. I knew that these were men that had done their tour of duty, and they had survived. Some you could tell were seasoned warriors by their hardened faces. As they were leaving, one of these seasoned soldiers looked me square in the eyes and said, "If you want to stay alive, forget everything you ever learned." Those departing words pierced my heart like an arrow; they were to stay with me throughout the war.

That night we were loaded on buses and taken from Bien Hoa airport to Long Bien Base Camp. We had to travel with the lights off and stay low to the floor, as we were told the enemy was infiltrating all areas. We arrived at Long Bien late in the evening. Each man grabbed his duffel bag and we were rushed into the barracks. The camp commander told us there was a blackout – no lights were allowed to be turned on, not even flash lights. Each of us had to find a bunk in the dark barracks. I located a top bunk, with no idea who the soldier below me was. An officer came in and warned us that if rockets and mortars were fired into our compound, we were to grab our mattress, hit the floor, and cover up with the mattress. I had no time to think about all that was happening. It all come about so fast, my mind whirled in a daze. I tried to relax, but the tension and fear were overwhelming. When my eyes finally started to close and sleep began to set in, an explosion suddenly awakened me.

The sky again was lit up with flares; gunfire was all around us. Within seconds there was another explosion, this one was in our compound. I jumped off my cot to the floor, and reached up for the mattress, but it had already been taken. I lay on the floor with no covering, no shelter. There was no room under the bunk beds, for others like myself had crawled to any space they could to find shelter.

Mortars and rockets continued to detonate within the compound. The sky lit up with a flash as each round hit. I thought my heart was going to burst; never had I known such fear as this. I thought if there was a hell, this was it. None of us had rifles, and some of us yelled out for them. However, soldiers outside rebuked us and told us to stay low and not to leave the barracks. I had visions of some enemy running through the door shooting us all as we hid without any weapons to defend ourselves.

The explosions never ceased that night, as the fighting raged around us. Not far from our barracks there was an ammo dump, a place where weapons and ammo were stored. A Vietcong sapper infiltrated our camp and set off an explosive charge that killed him and destroyed the ammo dump. Throughout the night and the next day the ammo exploded. This was my first twenty-four hours in Vietnam.

The next morning they still kept us within the barracks. I wrote a letter; I penned the fear that was in my heart onto paper: "There is no way that I can survive one year of this hell on earth. I will never be going home." It was as though I were writing my own eulogy. I never sent the letter; I was searching for answers while trying to piece together the puzzle my life had become. I started to think of my past: "Maybe this is recompense for all of the wrongs that I have committed, maybe this is my just reward…."

Chapter 2

My past life was one of heartaches and bitter changes, coming from a large family that had its fill of sorrows and break ups. As I remember my past, the earliest thought of childhood is a scene that has stuck with me throughout my life. It was a time when I was being placed in an institution for children, along with my brothers and sisters. I'm not sure why we were there except that my mother became ill. This place was cold, and had large rooms with beds set up on either side, just like a barracks. The people who watched over us were as cold as the building. I remember them locking my younger sister Theresa, hardly more than a toddler, in a closet for long periods of time because she would not quit crying.

Another picture that I have had in my mind (since childhood) is of me sitting by a window, looking out over a grassy hill that sloped down to a lake, and the beautiful trees that surrounded it. There was a man in a boat, fishing. It was a beautiful sight. It seemed out of my grasp, something that I would always see through a window, but never come to know in my life. I do not know why that scene has remained in my mind all through the years, but it has.

Much of my youth was spent in institutions. Tragedies seemed to keep my family from ever being together for more than a couple of years at a time. Even when we were together as a family, we never stayed in one place for long. We moved from town to town.

When I was in the first grade we were living in Detroit, and had to walk about a mile and a half to school. My brother Russ and I, on our way to school each day, had to cross a busy intersection. One morning the light was green for us to go, but as we were crossing, a truck ran through the intersection, striking us both. I remember seeing people standing around me as I lay in the street. It was a strange sensation; I don't remember feeling any pain, but I do remember the feeling that I was going to die. As young as I was, I could feel my life slipping away from me.

The next thing I remember is waking in the hospital. I don't know how many days I remained unconscious, but when I awoke, I had bandages over my head. My skull was fractured, and I had to stay in the hospital for a long period of time. My brother had lost some teeth, and was badly bruised from the accident. I had been in front of the truck when it hit us, knocking me into my brother, and then into the air. After the accident, I had a hard time comprehending things. School became difficult and I suffered with severe headaches. I became very insecure, and felt I was stupid because I could not understand things taught in the classroom.

Again we were sent to another institution. I was separated from my sisters, but was with my brothers. We slept in dorms, about six boys to a room. Each morning we were to clean the dorms before breakfast. The dining area was large and all four or five units of boys had meals together. The Catholic nuns, in charge of this institution, were strict. We didn't dare talk back to them, as they would not hesitate to crack us with the paddle.

This place didn't have any showers; instead, there were tubs, about six in a row. Each night we had to take a bath, one boy in each tub. There weren't any curtains separating the tubs, so there wasn't any privacy. The nuns would come in and scrub our hair, and then once a week, while sitting in the tub, we were given a tablespoon of cod liver oil. We were told that it was good for us, but each time I drank it I thought I would bring it right back up.

It was at this early age that I started to feel like just a number, someone without a purpose. There wasn't any love in these places, no affection, no one to sit down with me, like my mom would, and talk to me, or hug me. There was a seed of rebellion growing within, a bitterness taking root.

One day for lunch we were given rice pudding, something I detested. The nun they called "mother superior" came over and told me that I had to eat it. I refused. She pulled on my ear and told me that I would sit there until I did. I don't remember how long I sat there, but I was determined that I would not eat that pudding. I was only about nine years old, yet within I was becoming mean and spiteful.

The one joy I got out of this place was when our counselor, a young man, would come and teach us. He would take us into the woods and teach us things about nature. I enjoyed being in the woods; it seemed to draw me like a magnet. Every chance I had I would go into the woods, and if I couldn't be outside, I would look out my window at them. This counselor helped us build a small bridge over a stream, and I remember thinking what a great bridge it was. I felt so proud of this accomplishment. I would dream of that bridge, and see myself having a tree fort right next to it that I could live in and hide from the world of pain that I had come to know.

One morning I slipped out early and climbed the fence of the compound and ran away. I was missing my mom and dad, and wanted to see them. I didn't have any idea what to do next, or in which direction to go, so I just began walking down the road. Two surveyors took notice of me, and could tell that I was lost. I remember they took me to their home and asked me where I was headed. I told them I was looking for my dad. They had already contacted the police – I was frightened to return to the institution, and didn't know what was going to happen next. The men fed me some lunch and talked with me about the deer they would often see in the woods. I cheered up and stood by the window as one of the men pointed to a place where the deer roamed. I looked out the window toward the woods, wishing that my dad would come and get me. The police came and took me back to the home; I was taken into the main office where I sat waiting to see "mother superior." To my surprise, however, my dad came instead. He asked me why I ran away, and I told him that I just wanted to go back home, to be with him and mom. My dad hugged me, and that day he took my brother and I out for a few days.

I did not understand why we were separated through those years. I knew my mother suffered with health problems and she was often hospitalized. My dad worked for the railroad, and could not take care of us during the day. I know he did not want to put us in these institutions, but with so many children, he seemed to have no choice.

Chapter 3

When I left the Catholic institution after a year or so, our family moved into a house. My mother was still ill, but she worked hard at caring for us. Over the next few years we lived in different houses. In one home we had a fire in the basement when our parents were not home. My older sister and brother were watching us, when one of us smelled smoke. My brother Russ and I ran down into the basement and saw the blaze. We hurried everyone out of the house and no one was injured. We lost most of our belongings, however, and had to move again.

After a few years had passed, my dad decided to move us to a small town. I was about twelve years old. He found us a nice home in Gibraltar, Michigan. We settled in, and it seemed things were better. I still struggled in school and had a rebellious streak within, but I was starting to make friends. I had not had much of an opportunity in the past for any long-term friendships.

One cold January evening I went to a school dance. On my return home with some friends, I could see smoke coming out of the upstairs window of our house. I ran to the front door, but it was locked. I banged and banged until I saw my mother through the window, trying to reach the upstairs. I quickly ran to the back door and pushed my way in. The smoke was heavy and I could hardly breathe. My younger brothers and sisters ran down the steps, coughing and crying. My grandmother, who had just arrived that day from New Jersey, ran up the stairs because her grandson who had traveled with her from New Jersey was still upstairs. She never came back down. I tried to run up to find her, but I could not reach the top floor; the smoke was too heavy. I turned back.

My older sister's friend, who drove us home from the dance, wet a towel and put it around his face and ran up the steps. He came back down moments later dragging my grandmother behind him. The smoke had blackened her face, and she was unconscious. My young cousin from New Jersey was still upstairs, and I had no idea where my dad was.

It seemed like an eternity had passed before the fire department arrived. The firemen quickly rushed in and forced us all out. I kept yelling: "Where's my dad?" They pushed me back and told me that he was okay. One fireman ran up the steps and soon returned clutching my young cousin to his chest.

My dad died in the fire that night, and a few days later my grandmother perished from smoke inhalation. My young cousin survived. He was sleeping with his mouth close to his pillow, which helped save him.

I found out years later that my younger brother, Frank, was the last person to see my dad alive. He tried to reach my father in the fire, but my dad told him to get everybody out, and to look after the family. It was a tragic loss for us all. The fire left our family broken and crushed.

Chapter 4

My mother became ill from the tragic loss of her husband and her mother. As a result, my grandfather and grandmother, my father's parents, decided to separate us children and put us into different institutions. We were split up again, away from each other.

I ended up in a place that was for boys who had difficulties in life. Men who were studying to be Catholic priests ran this place. One such man disliked me, and found pleasure in seeing that my life was made miserable. I had very few clothes, and the clothes I had were all sewn to fit me. I was so skinny that I had my pant legs pegged; it was the style at that time. My first evening in the home, this man took out the sewn seams in my pants and left them hanging on the edge of my bed. I came in from dinner, and immediately felt sick to my stomach when I saw what he had done. The pants were not only baggy on me, but there were permanent marks all the way down the legs from the seams. I had to go to my first day of school looking like this, and I was laughed at from that day forward. I hated this place, and wanted out. My brother and I ran away a couple of times. The first time we took off, the police caught us about a week later.

There was another young boy who ran away with us; we knew him from another institution that we had been in. This boy was on the same floor as I. We had the same dorm counselor, the one that disliked me. When we were returned to the home, this man took us into the bathroom with the rest of the boys on our floor, and he had me take a belt and whip the other boy who ran away with me. Then I, too, had to drop my pants and let the other boy whip me, while all the other boys watched. I had never experienced such humiliation and shame. I had hatred inside for this counselor, this man who was studying to be a priest.

The second time my brother and I ran away, we took another kid with us. We headed to the area where we used to live. We didn't have any money, any food, or a place to sleep. My brother found some of his friends, and after a few days he left us. My friend and I were alone, with nowhere to go.

We decided we needed a car, so we tried to steal one. Neither of us knew how to drive, so we didn't go far before the police caught us. The boys' home would not take me back, so I was incarcerated in the juvenile center in Detroit, Michigan.

It was a hard place; counselors and kids alike were mean and brutal. Most kids were released within a week; however, I was there for many months. It was a time of loneliness and bitter resentment for me. I didn't receive any letters or visitors, and had no idea where my mother or brothers and sisters were. I wrote letters to relatives asking for some information, but I received no reply. Day in and day out, I looked out the window at what I thought was freedom. I thought of that man in the boat, that ever-fleeing dream of serenity. Like a painted picture that was ever in my mind, at times it tormented me, and at other times it was a ray of hope yet out of reach.

There was a lot of fighting in the youth home. A number of boys would often gang up on one person at a time. If we watched TV, we were not allowed to move or talk with anyone else. If caught, the counselors would have us stand on an imaginary line in the hall for hours without moving. Many times I stood on that line for hours on end. One counselor would make us kneel before him, then he would take his knuckles and crack us on the head a few times, then tell us to go stand on the line until he became tired. My heart hardened through the years of disappointment and sorrow; I was foul-mouthed and angry within.

One afternoon I was sitting with the other boys watching TV. I had a dirty piece of cloth about two inches long in my hand. I'm not sure what I was doing with it, but the counselor came over to me and told me to eat it. I said "no." He had a whistle on, and something that looked like a little whip made out of strips of vinyl. He started beating me with it until I fell to the floor. He demanded that I eat it; I refused. He finally gave up, and I had to stand on the line. There was one particular counselor who worked the evening watch who was very cruel. This man would have us all stand in a line facing him, and then he would put on a black leather glove and go down the line punching each one of us in the chest. If one of the boys cried, the rest of the youth were allowed to beat up on him. I learned to never shed a tear.

We had only one Ping-Pong table for thirty or more boys; you had to be good to play. I had been there for so long that I learned to play well. One night a youth I had defeated in a game did not like it, so he told the biggest boy in the unit that I had been playing "the dozens," as they called it. I don't know where the term originated, but it was a term used when someone talked about another boy's family in an evil way. The death of my father in the house fire was often mocked, causing me to get into fights. This day, though, I had said nothing, nor did I ever speak against someone's family. However, the big boy attacked me, and punched me in the face. To this day I don't know what happened, but the next morning I found myself locked up in isolation. They told me that I had gone crazy, that I had grabbed two ping-pong paddles and threatened anyone who came near me. They said I was like a mad man. I do not remember any of it. I think all the years of hurt and pain that had built up inside of me exploded into a fit of rage. What happened scared me; I didn't understand why I could not remember, and I wanted to go home. I wanted to be free from all of the sorrow and pain.

The only joy I found in this place was being able to work in the kitchen. It kept me busy and I was able to get out of the unit for a few hours. I worked with an older cook; he was a friendly man who took a liking to me. I remember him because he tried to encourage me to do right. He tried to teach me that life was valuable and that I should not have so much hatred within. I was a young, skinny little white boy filled with confusion and despair, and this older black man treated me as if I were a son. I looked forward to my time down in the kitchen because there I found someone who cared.

One day I decided to escape. I had gotten hold of about thirty belts from some of the other boys who wanted to help me escape, and I stored them under my cot. On certain days we were taken outside to play baseball. Surrounding the courtyard was a solid brick wall about eighteen feet high. The walls had security lights on them, and I thought I could lasso one of the lights, scale the wall, drop the belts to the other side, let myself down and be free. I had watched one other youth do it and succeed. The day of my planned escape, I was in line to go outside when a counselor came over to me, pulled me out of the line and searched me. Someone had turned me in. They found the bag of belts stashed in the raggedy baggy pants they dressed us in. They locked me up in isolation for about two weeks. I remember getting on my knees at night and crying, asking God to help me. One night I was praying and a counselor looked through my window; he didn't see me, so he burst through the door thinking I had escaped, only to find me praying on my knees. He shut the door quietly, and I just stayed on my knees and wept.

I wasn't allowed to work in the kitchen anymore because of my escape attempt. This was devastating for me. One day the cook came up to my unit, took me into a corner, and scolded me as he pulled my ear and asked me why I did such a stupid thing. I could see in his eyes that he was hurt and disappointed. I knew this man really wanted to help me, and I had ruined it, just as I had everything else.

Chapter 5

Months passed without a word from anyone. Then one day a man called me out and took me to a room for counsel. He was a kind man, and he told me that my mother had been in a hospital for a long time. She hadn't even known where I was until this time. I asked if I was going to be able to leave. He said he didn't know, but that he was planning to find out some information and would try to help me get released. I found out from him that if any relative would have come for me at any time, I could have been released.

A couple of weeks passed by and things remained the same. Then one Saturday as I was watching TV, the counselor came out holding someone's records. This was usually an indication that someone was being released. He called out a name, but I didn't pay attention because it was always someone else. Then he asked me if I was staying. It was my name that he had called. I was being released. It was hard to believe I was getting out. My Aunt Mary, my mother's sister, found out that I was in the youth home. I had never met her, and could not understand how she knew I was in the youth home. The only other relatives I knew lived in Michigan, and they were from my father's side. I knew they never thought too much of me, or seemed to care what happened to our family. However, my aunt took a Greyhound bus all the way from Salt Lake City, Utah, to come and take me to her home.

The day I was released, we boarded the Greyhound bus and headed back to Salt Lake City. My aunt not only came to get me, she also took my sister, Theresa, out of an institution for girls. I had not seen Theresa in more than a year.

The bus trip was long, but I was free. I knew nothing about the West, and I was fascinated when the bus reached the Rocky Mountains. I had never imagined that there could be a wonder of nature such as this. Salt Lake City is a city surrounded by mountains, a small city in comparison to Detroit. I settled into my aunt's home, and my cousins treated me like a brother.

I managed to meet some friends. They were mischievous like I was. I didn't get into any trouble with the law while I stayed in Salt Lake, but I did manage to be a nuisance. My aunt and uncle were very kind to my sister and me, and even though the house they lived in was small, they found room for us. This act of love and kindness was beyond all I had known in the past, outside of my immediate family. The day came when I found out that my mother was no longer in the hospital, and that I could go back to Michigan. I was fifteen years old when I left Utah to travel back to Detroit on a Greyhound bus.

My time back home was a time of running the streets, of going where I pleased. My mother tried her best to control us; I seldom listened. I was never disrespectful to my mother, but once outside of the home, I was on my own. We had to move in with other people because we couldn't afford a place of our own; I didn't get along well in this situation, so I decided to live in the streets. My brother and I would often find an abandoned vehicle to sleep in. Even on cold winter nights we would curl up in old trucks and try to stay warm. Finally my mother was able to get her own apartment, and we moved back in. My mother was dating, and there was talk of marriage. I was glad to see the joy restored in her life.

My brother came home one evening and told me that he was going to California with some friends. I begged him to let me go, and the five of us piled in an old Ford coupe with no hood over the engine, and with just seventy-five dollars between us, headed out west. We hustled people along the way, and stole gas and food to get us by. We were just outside of Amarillo, Texas, when the engine blew two pistons. We didn't know what to do, so we all hung out at the Greyhound bus depot. Stealing became a way of surviving. Somehow we ended up with some cash, and a teenager sold us an old Chevy for thirty-five dollars. When I think back, I believe he must have stolen it. We headed west again.

We finally made it to Los Angeles. The bus depot in Los Angeles was a large building where we could hang out unnoticed among the crowds. We would often go into the cafeteria and order food, and then just leave without being detected. This went on for days. Sometimes my brother and the older guys would leave my friend and me at the bus depot while they took off in the car. We asked people for spare change so we could purchase tickets for the all-night movie theater, then we went into the theater, found seats in the rear, and slept.

One day we took the car to Santa Barbara, California, and while we were there the clutch went out, so we abandoned the car. We were hungry and without shelter.

I was fifteen years old and standing in the Santa Barbara Salvation Army's food line, waiting to get a bed and a meal. We told them that we were traveling together as a band, and that our car broke down. I remember lying in the cot that night, looking at all the down-and-out men. I was just a lad; these men were older – more than twice my age. Some looked as though they hadn't taken a shower or shaved in months. I knew most were drunkards with nowhere to go. I couldn't imagine ending up like them, and I despised the thought of it.

That night a few of my friends slipped out the back door to go hang out in town. When they returned, we let them in through the fire escape, but the alarm went off. The next morning, after breakfast, we were asked to leave.

We all managed to get back to LA, where I again found myself hanging out at the bus depot – alone, without food or money. I decided I would hitchhike back home, so with a quarter in my pocket I headed out. I hitchhiked down Route 66, then north toward Michigan. I don't remember how many days it took, but when I returned home I still had the same quarter in my pocket.

Chapter 6

I was glad to be home, though I was still uneasy, and had no direction for my life. My mother married and we moved to Monroe, Michigan, to a large, older home on Lake Erie. I liked this home, and enjoyed very much watching the sun come up on the lake. I missed my friends, however, so I began to hitchhike about thirty miles each day just to hang out at the pool hall.

Tom, the man my mother married, was kind and patient with us. He took on a big responsibility. He took good care of my mother and my younger brothers and sisters. I just wanted a place to hang out, and wasn't willing to abide by any house rules.

It wasn't long before a group of us decided to head out west again; this time in an old 1959 Ford hardtop convertible. There were five of us. We loaded all of our stuff in the trunk and headed west, but en route we found that the trunk was jammed, and would not open. Needless to say, by the time we reached the west coast, we all smelled pretty bad, not having changed our clothes in days. In LA we were able to get the trunk open and were grateful for a change of clothing.

The five of us traveled by car up and down the coast. Whenever we could, we'd siphon gas out of parked cars, steal food, and run out of restaurants without paying. We traveled to San Francisco, hungry and again without shelter. While there, we met a teenager who told us about a place where all kinds of "freaky" people were hanging out. He sent us to the cross streets of Haight and Asbury. It was evening when we found it. I had never seen anything like it before; hundreds of young people walking the streets in tie-dye shirts, long hair, and beads. Until then, I had never heard of "hippies". This particular place in San Francisco was the start of the movement, and we found ourselves right in the middle of it.

There was a bulletin board posted at a little church in the area. On the board there were addresses listed for people to go who had no place to stay. We went to one of these places, an old three-story house on Clayton Street. The house was filled with these longhaired people. I remember there was a coffin in the living room that one guy slept in. The air was filled with smoke from the marijuana that was passed around. Others were spaced out on drugs I had never even heard of. The older hippies cooked big pots of soup, and gave it to us with a slice of bread. While there, we would go out and steal food to bring back to the house as if we were doing our part. It was all so weird and strange to me.

One night they let an old man in who had been living in the streets. He was sitting next to me during mealtime when suddenly he started to shake and scream. He was crying out that spiders were crawling all over him. I had never seen anyone with *DT's before. It scared me, and I wanted to get away from there. We all left and headed to Hollywood. In Hollywood we were able to get a studio room apartment, and all packed in together. It wasn't long, however, before tensions set us on edge, and I decided I was going to head home. I stuck out my thumb and headed back down Route 66. I was now sixteen, nearing my seventeenth birthday.

(*abbreviation for delirium tremens, *a mental and nervous disorder accompanied by violent tremblings and terrifying hallucinations, usually caused by prolonged and excessive drinking of alcoholic liquor.)*

Chapter 7

Back in Michigan, I hung out with some friends from school, drinking and causing trouble wherever we could. One night we were all partying back in the forest. Some teenagers we had never met showed up at the party. I ended up in a fight with one of them, and while rolling on the ground in the scuffle; someone hit him with a bottle. He was hurt and everyone quickly left. Later that evening the police pulled us over. I was arrested for hitting the boy with the bottle, even though I did not do it. I was charged with felonious assault, and spent weeks in jail waiting for my court date.

My life seemed an endless cycle of trouble. Before I was arrested, I had visited an Army recruiter thinking I might join, but did not pursue it. While in jail, my mother talked to the Army recruiter, who in turn talked with the judge. The judge told me that if I would go into the armed forces, I would be released; but if not, I would spend time in jail. I told him that I would join the Army, thinking that I would at least have some free time before I left. The judge then ordered me to be at the recruiter's office by six a.m. the next morning.

At six in the morning I was taken to the recruiter's office by my family, and from there to Fort Wayne in Detroit. At Fort Wayne I was to receive my physical and be inducted into the Army. It was a long day, but by late afternoon I was sworn in as a soldier of the United States Army.

That night we were all loaded onto a train that would take us to Fort Knox, Kentucky, where we were to go through basic training. At Fort Knox I experienced my first days of military life. My first encounter was with a foul-mouthed drill sergeant who was intent on harassing us all. Any wrong move on our part and we learned quickly what it meant to "push dirt," a term used for doing push-ups. My first few days of training I seemed to do a lot of that.

Our group was made up of young men from all parts of the country, most of us just seventeen and eighteen years old. There were those who were drafted, those who joined, and those, like me, who weren't really given a choice. The first few weeks were a time of utter clumsiness. Marching in unison was difficult; left face, right face – most of us made the wrong face. The drill sergeants had their work cut out for them. Up at five, we had to pass inspection by five-thirty. After inspection we had to run to breakfast, after breakfast began our training.

Most of our training at first seemed to be marching and running. I remember one hill we had to march up was called the heartbreak hill. After marching up this hill, we felt as though our hearts would explode. Training became more intense as the weeks went by.

Talk of the war, and who would go, was a nightly conversation in the barracks. We trained with rifles, grenades, and other weapons that were to prepare us for battle. After basic training, we all had to go through eight more weeks of advanced training.

I found out that I was going to Fort Leonard Wood in Missouri for my advanced individual training. I was to go through Combat Engineering training, and I had no idea what that involved. When I arrived in Missouri, I found the training even more difficult than boot camp. I was taught how to mine-sweep, use explosives, and train for jungle warfare. Still, most of us did not know if we were going to Vietnam or if we were to be shipped off to some European country.

The day the orders came in, I was told that I would be going to Vietnam. I had no idea what to expect, except that I was going to fight a war in which I knew nothing about. The drill sergeant told me that because I was so small, I would probably be a tunnel rat. I didn't know much about it, except that it was very dangerous. The war seemed to have no real purpose – we were told that we were stopping the spread of communism.

I went home for a month's leave, in which I quickly found my old friends, and spent the time partying, trying not to think about what was ahead of me. The day came to leave, my family took me to the airport, and I kissed my mom good-bye.

I flew to Oakland, California, with orders to report to a staging base where military personnel were being shipped out to South East Asia. Oakland military compound was like a warehouse of men – Army, Navy, Marines, and Air Force all crowded into this one base. I reported to a certain section of Army personnel, then we were separated like cattle and assigned bunks to await the day of departure. It was a lonely time of anxious anticipation. Every face seemed to reflect a quiet fear of the unknown. Most were just young men being shipped off to a war on the other side of the world that none of us really understood. It seemed like we were all just a number, an expendable commodity in the hands of a cold-hearted monster. I thought to myself, "Who cares if I go to war – outside of my family, who cares if I live or die?" It all made no sense to me, and it added to my dread of the unknown.

Chapter 8

My life seemed to flash by me the first few days in Vietnam. The third day in the country was a day of induction, and introduction to this strange world. I quickly learned that Vietnam was a country that had known the horrors of war for many years, and that the people lived with suffering day in and day out. Things were quieter the day of induction; however, fighting could still be heard off in the distance. I met some of the friends I had trained with in the States and was hoping that I would be sent with at least one of them to my assignment. Instead, I was separated with a group of men who were all strangers to me.

The commanding officer told us that we would be going by convoy to the Tay Ninh province, a place well-known for the fierce battles that had taken place there. The convoy was made up of supply trucks, tanks, and troop carriers. It was an all-day journey through a strange countryside. The people along the road seemed to ignore us, except for those trying to sell goods to us along the way. It was a bizarre land to me. Barefooted children taunted and teased us at every stop. Women with wide-brimmed, triangle-shaped straw hats walked along the road carrying loads that looked much too heavy for their frail bodies. Everyone had a look of suspicion. In training we were told not to trust anyone; they said the Vietcong could be anywhere. They informed us that the Vietcong would work in the fields during the day, and at night set land mines and booby traps and also infiltrate military compounds. I couldn't imagine what it would be like to fight these people, or even why we would want to. I remembered our training, the warnings of a savage people that we were to hate – "gooks" they were called by those who prepared us for this day. However, I was seeing only frail, humble people trying to live out their lives in the midst of a bitter and confusing war.

We arrived at the Tay Ninh camp in the evening. Again, we were put into an induction barracks. I quickly checked out my new surroundings, assuming this would be the place I would spend my tour of duty. The next day, a small group of us was separated from the others. We were informed that our destination was another place called Dau Tieng.

That night, soldiers who had been in the country for a while instructed us about our new destination. It was nicknamed Rocket City. These men seemed to enjoy putting fear into our hearts, knowing we were new and inexperienced. Dau Tieng, we found, was a compound that was close to the Ho Chi Mien trail, which was used by the enemy to transport supply from the North. Dau Tieng was on the enemies hit list, because it was so close to their positions.

We traveled by a much smaller convoy to Dau Tieng; however, we were traveling with more firepower. The fear in my heart was intensified as we traveled toward Dau Tieng. There was an eerie feeling on this road – thick jungles and rubber plantations seemed to have eyes. I knew that this was a dangerous place. I thought that we were entering the gates of hell.

On arriving, I was assigned to an engineer unit. They took me to a tent that slept about twelve men, and assigned me to a cot. My first job was to construct a thin wooden frame over my cot that could hold a mosquito net. Malaria was a problem in Vietnam along with other tropical diseases.

A few days passed without incidence. At our new post we worked during the day, and at night played cards and talked. A three-foot wall of sand bags to help protect us from shrapnel surrounded our tent. There were also bunkers that were dug into the ground and sandbags that made up the roof.

One morning we were working on a warehouse. I was on the roof when the first mortar round hit. The explosion was close by. Everyone on the roof scurried to the ground, and I, too, quickly jumped from the roof. I followed the others to a bunker close-by, and found myself curled up in a small corner. The mortars and rockets hit all around us. They lasted about half an hour. Some soldiers joked and laughed. They were used to the harassment from the enemy. It was new for me, and the sound of the rockets whistling through the air put a shiver up my spine.

Weeks went by and I, like the others, seemed to have gained an instinct as to when the enemy would hit us. Even late in the night, my ears seemed to be tuned in to the thumping sound, off in the distance, of the mortars leaving the tubes shot off from the enemy's position. Many nights I woke up and ran to a nearby bunker yelling, "incoming," before one round hit the ground. Often, early in the morning, our platoons were called to stand in formation. This was not a good move on the part of the commanding officer, as it made us a good target for the enemy. They would shoot the rockets into the compound when we were lined up, and the whole formation of men would scramble, trying to find a nearby bunker. Men died because of this unwise decision; still we were ordered to stand in these formations, unaccompanied by the commanding officer.

There was a growing unrest between the men and the leaders. While I was in this outfit, more than once, a grenade was thrown at the commanding officer's tent. This was called "fragging," a term used throughout Vietnam. There were a number of incidences in the war where someone had killed or wounded an officer by "fragging."

One night I was up late walking through the compound when an explosion went off. I yelled "incoming," thinking it was a mortar attack, and everyone woke and ran to the bunkers. However, there were no other explosions that followed. The next day we were told that someone tried to "frag" the commanding officer's tent. A few days later I was approached by an officer who read me my rights, and then he told me that I was under suspicion, since I was around the facility during the time of the explosion. I knew I did not do it, so I didn't fear any response by headquarters. I never heard another word on the matter, and within days we received a new captain, one that wisely did not have us fall out for formations in the morning.

After I had been there nearly five months, a convoy brought in some new recruits. One particular man I will never forget. His name was Johnson, a young black man from Alabama. He bunked next to me. There was something different about him, which set him apart from the rest of us. He had a contagious smile, and unbelievable joy seemed to pour out of his life – something I had never known. It was different; as though it was not of this world. We became friends. He told me he was a Baptist. I had no idea what that was at the time, and it was not his church affiliation that set him apart. He said he loved the Lord. I thought it strange at first, but soon found his faith was strong and sure. No matter how we tried to get him to accompany us in our partying and carousing, he would not give in. He would just smile and say that he could not do such things because he loved the Lord. He never told me I was a dirty rotten sinner; never condemned me. He didn't have to – I had enough guilt in my heart for the whole army. He was the first true Christian I had ever met. Even though I did not understand his faith, I knew it was real. I thought it to be out of my reach, and even though he would tell me Jesus loved me, I still didn't understand such a commitment as his. I look back now, and I can truly say that he was a walking sermon; he touched my life and planted a seed that would one day take root. Even when we were attacked, he seemed to have a peace that did not waiver or fear.

The night attacks increased, and our perimeters were probed constantly by sniper fire. It was the evening of the Fourth of July, 1968, when the camp was ground-assaulted by the enemy. I was on perimeter guard duty. My bunker was being fired upon by sniper fire. The enemy fired about five hundred rockets and mortar rounds into our compound before they made the ground assault. The sky was lit up with flares, and tracers filled the air. The fighting was heavy. Not far from my bunker the Vietcong breached our perimeter. They started setting off explosions inside the camp. The fighting grew fierce as the night went on. It was difficult to know where to look, because the enemy was now in front and behind. The command headquarters sent more soldiers to help us hold the perimeter. It became difficult to distinguish who was who. We called in air support, helicopter gun ships, and a plane that was nicknamed "puff the dragon," which was equipped with about four or five mini guns on the right side of the plane. Each gun was able to fire six thousand rounds per minute. This plane swept the outside of our perimeter.

Morning came, though it seemed it would never arrive. Bodies were scattered everywhere. One Vietcong was still squatting just outside one of our bunker doors. Though he was dead, he still looked alive. He was about to pull the pin on a grenade right before he was killed. His finger was still in the ring of the pin, and he was strapped with sacho charges all around his waist. Another second, and he would have wiped out everyone in that bunker. A strange fear seemed to sweep the whole camp. We didn't know if there were still any enemy left within the compound, so we had to make a sweep of the whole camp.

Many soldiers died that night, and the reality of the war was rooted in my life forever. My life could never be the same. Though just eighteen, I lost all youth and innocence that day. Seeing others as young as I was – dead – and knowing that it could have been me crushed my heart and I felt as if I had died, too, along with them.

Who knows what war is like but a veteran? Who can say they understand the hurt, pain, bitterness, and confusion that take root in any soldier's life that has tasted battle? The only ones are the innocent men, women, and children that are caught in the middle of man's ultimate rage.

When I saw the enemy dead, some even younger than I, I didn't know how to feel. It was as if it had all been a bad dream. I longed to go home, to feel the cool Michigan winds, and to stand by the shorelines of the Great Lakes. The heat of the tropics was difficult to live with, along with the insects that were a constant thorn in the flesh. The monsoons came with the heavy rains. I didn't know that such torrential rainfalls were possible, and wondered how we were able to live through them.

Chapter 10

One evening I was on perimeter duty; the night was quiet except for a few rats scurrying around my feet in the bunker. The next morning I went back to the tent and laid down on my cot. I was allowed to sleep for four hours before I had to go back on duty. It was a nice cool morning for Vietnam, a good time to rest. A few of my friends passed through the tent, made some joking remarks to me, and then I was left alone. My eyes were closing. I was about to sleep, when I heard a voice say: "Get up, get out." My heart was beating fast; I felt as though it were about to come out of my chest. There was no one in the tent but me. Again I heard the voice: "Get up, get out."

I quickly jumped to my feet and ran outside the tent, heading for the nearest bunker. Before I made it, however, the first rocket hit close behind me. Shrapnel flew everywhere. I made it to the bunker, and waited out the attack. When I left the bunker I discovered that the first rocket had hit the tent. It exploded right in front of my cot. Everything I owned was shredded. My steel locker was twisted and shattered by the explosion and shrapnel. My cot was but a shredded rag. I thought of the strange voice, it's warning, and of my life having been spared. To this day I don't know if it was an audible voice or from within; all I know is that it saved my life.

That day was strange for me; I didn't know what to think. When night came I could hardly sleep, all that had happened haunted me like a bad dream. I kept thinking about being in that cot and not responding to the strange voice. I thought about God, and wondered why He would speak to me. I started to think that maybe it was my own mind, my own intuition, or a sixth sense, but nothing could explain what had occurred to me that day. I didn't tell anyone about the voice; the guys all thought I was just 'lucky.' That moment, however, that brief encounter with eternity, planted another seed. Within my soul I wanted to know why that warning spoke to my heart.

Days went by with the usual attacks. I seemed to always be one step ahead of the shrapnel that ripped through everything. Once, while riding in a truck, a round hit right behind us as we were driving. Another time I was trying to find cover with a fellow soldier behind some stacks of airstrip material. One of the incoming rounds hit almost at our heels as we were going for cover. Neither one of us was hurt, and we just laughed nervously. Another time I was in the chow line when mortars hit. There was no place to run, so we lay prone on the ground. Shrapnel hit me in the head, but we were far enough away from the initial impact that it felt like bee stings. Not even a scratch was left from that particular incident.

One day a group of us were assigned to go and repair a bridge that the enemy had damaged with explosives. We arrived early in the morning, and our first task was to mine-sweep the area, then we could start repairing the bridge. By late afternoon we were finished. We didn't realize that the Vietcong were in the hills watching us.

They started firing mortars and rockets at our position. I was on the bridge when the first one hit. I quickly jumped over the side and crawled under the bridge. It didn't take long to realize that they were trying to hit the bridge and destroy what we had just repaired. I rapidly crawled out from where I was hiding and headed toward one of the company trucks. The officer that was hiding under it yelled at me, saying there was no room. I ran as fast as I could to a low spot in the field that was covered with thorn bushes. I jumped into the middle of them, hoping that a sniper would not see me. The thorns pierced my skin as the sweat and dirt rolled down my face. I was frozen with fear, thinking the next mortar or rocket would land in this patch of brush I was lying in. The firing ceased when a helicopter gun ship cleared the area with machine gun fire. We headed back to the camp, and that evening the enemy blew the bridge.

Chapter 11

I hated being where I was. I wanted to be in the jungles with the ground troops. I didn't like being in the compound like a bunch of sitting ducks. I wanted to be out where the fighting was. So I extended my tour for six more months. That way, I was allowed to choose where I wanted to go. I chose the Eleventh Cavalry, nicknamed "Black Horse," because of their regiment patch: a black pony with a slash through the middle of the patch. I picked this outfit because I had watched them many times, riding on their tanks and APC that were called gun ships. They looked like a tough breed, always dirty-faced from the dust and dirt kicked up from traveling on tracks. They had a name for putting fear in the enemy. I thought this was where I wanted to be. My commanding officer told me I was crazy, and that I would probably be killed within the first week. I was given a thirty-day leave to go home, after which I was to return to Vietnam.

It was good to be home and to see my family. I missed the house on the beach and was glad to be able to watch the sun rise on the lake again. The war was not mentioned, however; it was as though it didn't exist. People in America seemed immune to it, even though the nightly news broadcast the fighting and suffering that was going on. Except for the protesters in the colleges and those who had sons and daughters in the war, the rest of the American public seemed apathetic. I felt as though I were in a carnival, in the midst of a country of people who just wanted to play, and to live their lives out in selfish ambition while the rest of the world suffered.

America – the home of the brave, the land of the free. The brave were losing their lives in the jungles of Vietnam, and the free were enjoying their freedom.

My thirty-day leave was just a time to party along with the rest. I tried to drown out the fact that I had to return. I even thought of going AWOL. When the time came to go back, however, I boarded my plane and wondered if I would return home in a body bag.

As soon as I reached Vietnam I had to report to my new outfit. I had no idea what to expect or how I would be received. I traveled from Saigon by convoy to my destination. It was not difficult finding my outfit. I reported to headquarters, and right away the company commander came out to meet and welcome me; I felt relieved. This man seemed different, like he was in touch with his men. I remember my first day there because when mail call came, one young Puerto Rican soldier received about four hundred letters. The next day he received about the same. His whole village wrote him. I thought it was wonderful. I never received much mail. My mother wrote, and that was about it. I was always glad, though, to hear from her and to find out that things were going well at home.

My new outfit was different; the whole atmosphere was not what I was accustomed to. There were many Puerto Ricans that hung out together. One thing I remember about them was their close friendships, and that they liked to sing. They would often stand outside the barracks and harmonize with each other, and they were good at it. The black soldiers also had their groups, as did the "heads" and the "juicers," terms used to distinguish the soldiers who smoked pot and those who drank. I fell into the category of heads. Smoking pot became a way of life for me, an escape from reality.

My first duty with my new outfit was minesweeping, clearing the roads and fields of any land mines that the enemy would plant into the ground at night. I became good at finding them. It was dangerous, because the mines were sometimes booby-trapped. If we tried to remove them after disarming them, there was always the possibility that another explosive underneath would be set off by pulling up the first mine. We always had to watch out for all kinds of traps and explosives. The Vietcong were good at using anything they could find to make homemade mines. Even the American bombs that were dropped from planes but did not detonate were used as traps.

One morning we were called out to clear a field because some mines had been placed there by the Vietcong. While clearing, a young boy approached me; he was holding a grenade in his hand. My heart started beating fast, because I knew that children were also used in the war to kill American troops. Many unsuspecting soldiers lost their lives because of the traps and grenades children had used. I saw fear reflected in his face as he approached, and I quickly turned toward him with my rifle pointing straight at him. He dropped the grenade and ran in fright. I soon discovered that he had found the grenade and wanted to give it to me. I felt a sadness in my heart that I could not trust even children, and the thought of shooting that boy plagued my mind.

Headquarters started sending us out on ambush patrols in the evenings. We would find a spot in the jungles or along a trail where we thought there would be enemy activity, then we would set up an ambush position, hoping to trap the enemy and get them in a cross fire. One night we pulled ambush patrol, but some village girls located us, and brought out some whisky and pot. Within a short amount of time, the whole patrol was stoned or drunk, and everyone was passed out. I awoke late in the evening, and found not one soldier awake. It was frightening, for if the enemy found us we would have never escaped. None of us seemed to know what we were fighting for. Vietnam was a corrupt government, and the common people suffered much because of it. The Vietcong tortured and killed many villagers for not assisting them, and the South Vietnamese troops did the same to villagers who helped or were suspected of helping the Vietcong. Even the American troops disliked the villagers; no one could be trusted, and everyone was suspected of being a Vietcong or an informant.

The drug culture in the U.S. was growing, and new troops brought in new music and new drugs. The morale was low, and the separation between troops became distinct – those that belonged to the new movement, and those that didn't. One thing remained constant, however, that in a fight we all stuck together.

We didn't like to fight alongside the South Vietnamese, as they were not trusted in battle by the American troops.

The American soldiers, however, would watch out for one another. There was no prejudice out in the field. The fight was against the enemy – our lives or theirs.

We went out on frequent patrols. One day we were patrolling a particularly dangerous area. I was on the last A-Cav (armored personnel carrier), when I noticed a group of men coming out of the jungle. They seemed surprised to come across our unit. It was a strange, almost eerie situation. I felt such an eerie feeling. These men were heavily armed. They were dressed in ragged South Vietnamese uniforms, however I noticed that they were barefooted, which was unusual for the South Vietnamese Army. They slowly walked past my track, and my eyes caught the stare of the last man in their position. It seemed like we were caught in a stare-down with each other. I couldn't get my eyes off of him – it felt as though he was staring a hole right through me, and I him. I could see fear and hatred in his eyes. We never quit staring at each other until they had faded into the jungle. My machine gun was pointed in their direction and my heart was pumping with adrenaline. I knew within that they were Vietcong.

A few minutes after they disappeared into the bush we received a radio call that an enemy patrol dressed as South Vietnamese troops was in our area. That man was my age – two teenagers facing each other down with a hatred neither of us probably would ever understand. I wonder today if he is still alive, and if he remembers my eyes as I remember his.

Soon after, we were ordered to move our base camp to Quan Loi, near An Loc, a village close to the Cambodian border. It was a hot spot. There was much fighting within this area. Quan Loi was a remote border camp, surrounded by jungles and rubber plantations. The people seemed different; the atmosphere was tense, the heat and humidity added to the uneasy mood that seemed to permeate the air. There was a village in the middle of our base camp. Our perimeter was built right around it. This village was under our care and protection, but we also knew that it was an easy place for the Vietcong to slip in and out of unnoticed. We were often hit with mortars and rockets, and our perimeter was constantly probed.

After a few weeks there, we were hit with a ground attack. They breached our line, blew up a few A-Cavs, and we lost some men. After that night, our perimeter became a free-fire zone, meaning that when we were on guard duty we could open fire whenever we thought the need. When on duty, this became a way of killing the monotony. We would fire flares all night, and shoot our grenade launchers as a contest to see who could shoot the farthest. Hand grenades were tossed out into the perimeter, and machine gun and rifle fire became a nightly occurrence.

We were not in base camp long before they sent us out on search and destroy missions. These excursions would last for weeks on end. Traveling through the jungles sitting on top of our tanks and A-Cavs was difficult. At night we would circle our tanks and A-Cavs like a wagon train, then put out the trip flares and barbed wire as a night perimeter. We also set claymore mines, trip mines that are set off by a hand device that shoot out thousands of B.B. type metal balls that destroy whatever happens to be in range. Sometimes the enemy would sneak up in the night and turn them toward our troops. When set off, they would shoot back at us instead of toward the enemy. Our solution to this was to paint the back of the mines white so we could see them in the night. That way if we could no longer see the white, we would not set them off.

Trooper on Patrol

The Wild One

Cooling off

Going to the Bush

Chapter 12

My first firefight in the jungles came on my first time out. We were in the thick of the jungle when we came across the enemies' compound. They had dug tunnels under the ground that connected with each other. We were right in the middle of this compound when they hit us with all they had. RPG's (Rocket propelled grenades) were fired at us, some hitting our tanks. I was on a 60-caliber machine gun; I just kept firing and kept my head low. The track across from me was hit. I could see one of our men bleeding. I knew we were in trouble. Helicopters and gun ships soon arrived and gave us air support. Fire and smoke charged the air. We pushed into their positions and soon took over. Many of the Vietcong escaped through an intricate network of tunnels. They sent a few men down in the tunnels to clear them, but most of the enemy had disappeared. My heart was rapidly beating, my adrenaline was high, and I felt a strange sense of boldness. Like most combat soldiers, there is a sense of fear, but one becomes accustomed to the fight. It is a strange thing within man that gives him the strength to carry on in such situations. Things I thought I could never face became not only a reality, but also a daily way of life.

In the enemies' camp, we found a large stash of weapons and rice. We set plastic explosives to them and destroyed them so they could never be used again. Medi-vac helicopters came in and took the dead and wounded out. We finished our clearing of the camp and went on.

Nighttime in the jungles was uneasy, being in the midst of enemy territory; any movement or sound would put a chill up the spine. The ants, leeches, scorpions, spiders and snakes were a round-the-clock unwanted host of the jungles. There was a snake we nicknamed "the five step snake" – it was the bamboo viper. Stories were told that if someone was bit, they could take only about five steps before they died. This little snake was difficult to see, as its color matched the leaves of the bamboo. One day we were set up in a perimeter. Everyone was at ease, taking rest, writing letters, or just sitting around talking. Across the perimeter, I noticed a young black soldier quickly jump to his feet, grab an M-60 Machine gun, and start firing at something near him. We ran over to see, but the only thing left of the little snake was his head, hanging from a small twig on a bush. The snake had crawled onto the soldier's blanket while he was resting. Seeing the snake, he panicked and started firing. It was hard to imagine using such firepower from an M-60 to kill a snake.

Out in the Bush

Phil a fellow brother in arms, I am on the M-50 gun behind him.

That same night within the perimeter, I was on guard when I heard movement out in front of us. Before I knew it, I saw a flash. An RPG was fired at our track, but it missed and hit a track behind me. We quickly responded, and the quiet night was shattered by the battle that ensued. As quickly as it started it seemed to be over. The RPG's hit a few tracks, and a number of our men were hurt. The Medi-vac choppers came and took them out. I often thought about being wounded and having to be shipped out – sent home, never to return. The fear of being shipped out in a body bag was a haunting reminder of the reality of war.

In the jungles, when we went out in search of enemy positions, it wasn't long before we found one. The twenty-fifth infantry assisted us in this; these guys were a tough breed. On one occasion as they searched the camp looking for tunnels, I was searching through some of the underbrush, and came across two VCs that were lying side by side. Mini guns from the choppers had hit them. What was left of them was a horrible sight. I stood there for a moment wondering what their lives had been like, who was waiting for them back home, and if they had wives or girlfriends.

It was all so insane, a madness that was impossible to understand. We found more bodies; also some VCs were captured and taken as prisoners. We found one tunnel that was being used as a hospital. The equipment they had been using was old and outdated. Bags filled with what looked like heroin were found. We thought that it may have been used as a painkiller for the wounded. I was standing with some of the twenty-fifth infantry by some of the dead VC when one of the soldiers pulled out his knife, cut the ear off of one of the dead and put it into his pocket. I, too, got caught up with this insanity, setting a dead VC up against a tree, and placing our regiment patch between his teeth so that when he was found by the VC they would know what outfit had been there. We placed a beer can in one hand and a cigarette butt in another. I remember we found something like a wallet in his pocket, and in it were some black and white photos. One was of a young teenage girl; I think it may have been his girlfriend. I could not get that picture out of my mind. I didn't understand the turmoil inside of me – one minute I felt compassion, the next, hatred.

Our outfit was sent back to the main camp for a time of recuperation. Back at camp we worked filling sand bags, repairing our equipment, and pulling guard duty at night. The second platoon was sent out on a routine patrol. They were ambushed and some returned in body bags.

The constant nagging feeling of being the next to be killed weighed heavily on my heart, as I know it did others. No one ever talked about it. When someone was killed, we silently grieved and went on as if it had not happened. I remember waking one night in a drenching sweat, thinking about death and hell. I knew within that I was a lost soul. I wanted to know if God was real, and if there was such a place called heaven. All I could think about was a judgment for my sins. I tried to brush it off, hide it deep within, but it was like a cancer eating away at my soul. I attended a church service back at camp, my first and only one. I remember the preacher praying that we would go out that week and come back with reports of a large body count (the number of enemy killed). I thought to myself, "if this is Christianity, I want nothing to do with it."

I started smoking more weed, trying to numb the feelings I felt inside. I never heard too much from home. I seared myself from even thinking that there was such a place as home. My six months of extension was close to being up; I don't know why, but I extended for another six months. I was given another thirty-day leave to go home.

Those thirty days were spent getting high; I did not want to return to the war. I thought for sure that if I went back to Vietnam I was going to be a causality of war, though in a sense I already was, mentally.

I traveled back to San Francisco to return back to Asia, but missed my plane. I was nineteen and so alone and scared. Instead of trying to catch another flight, I went to a military hospital. The fear within was eating me up; I just wanted to talk with someone, and I thought if I could find anyone who would understand, it would be there. I was escorted to a counselor, who I thought would listen to me, but he didn't really pay any attention. I quickly realized that I was just a nuisance, and was wasting his time. I returned to camp and flew out the next day.

Chapter 13

Back in Vietnam, I realized that at least for now this was my home; this was what I had come to know for almost two years. There seemed to be no life outside of this. I was soon sent back out into the jungles, and became good at minesweeping. I seemed to have a knack for finding them.

One day I was sweeping a road when I picked up a reading. I didn't feel like bending down and probing the ground to find anything, and presumed it was just some metal fragments that so often were scattered throughout the region. I kicked the dirt to see, and the tip of my boot uncovered a metal object. It was a tank mine and the tip of my boot was up against the detonating device. It should have gone off, but for some strange reason it didn't. I dug the mine up, but was shaken from the experience. I knew that my foolish assumption could have cost me my life and others around me. I was much more careful after that.

Another time our squadron was called out for a large campaign, a big push into the jungles to locate a concentration of enemy encampments. We had to minesweep a road on the way toward our objective. It was slow going because the convoy was made up of tanks, A-Cavs, and equipment, and the place was often mined, so we had to be extra careful. We came to a crossroads where some military police were waiting to go by. They demanded us to let them through, but we told them they had to wait until the road was cleared. They didn't like to be told what to do – their vehicle was a large, armored personnel carrier, not like ours, and it had large wheels and was easy to maneuver. They decided to go around us by driving on the grassy slope alongside of us. They went about twenty yards past me when I heard the explosion. Metal debris flew everywhere. We quickly hit the ground until the smoke cleared. They hit a large mine, the vehicle was totally destroyed, and I don't think any one of them made it out alive. We continued on and cleared the road; so went another day in Vietnam.

In the jungles again it was slow-going, as usual. Each night we set up like a wagon train, put out our trip flares and some barbed wire. Snipers would shoot into our circle, but nothing heavy was happening. Each day we pushed farther in. The jungle became thicker and the going was rough. It was an eerie feeling to be this far into the jungle, not knowing what lie ahead.

One day, about midday, we came upon a downed helicopter. It had burst into flames from enemy fire and was lying on its side amongst the trees. We stopped there and circled again for the night. I knew something was up; there was an uncertain, unearthly feeling in the air. Our commanding officers told us that a Vietcong was captured not far from our position. The Vietcong prisoner informed our leaders that we were just outside the perimeter of a large enemy underground bunker complex. That night we all stayed awake in nervous anticipation of what was to happen the next morning.

We moved in by early dawn, and ended up in the center of the complex before we even knew it. The enemy opened up on us; there were bullets flying from every direction. I jumped to the ground with the infantry and started laying out a field of fire in front of us. Within minutes one of our sergeants was hit. He was not wounded badly, so we bandaged him and he kept going. Our lead tank hit some of the worst fire. The enemy was moving all around in front of them. One of the gunners was hit, and the sergeant of that tank carried him to safety and was shot in the process. He didn't stop. He went back to his tank and started firing his machine gun. The VC was so close that they were trying to climb up on the vehicle. The sergeant was hit a few more times and still would not quit. Snipers were in the trees trying to pin us down. One of the infantry was wounded and calling for help, so off went four or five others 'grunts' to rescue him. I tried to go with them, but our sergeant made me hold my position. The fighting raged all day, as we cleared each bunker. We threw hand grenades down the tunnels, and then some would go in and check them out. It was a large underground complex; there seemed to be hundreds of entrances. These tunnels seemed to go for miles, like an endless chain – a maze beneath our feet.

By evening the fighting ceased. The dead and the wounded were taken out by helicopter. Much of the enemy had escaped through the tunnels, leaving behind a large cache of weapons. We also found a huge stash of rice. I couldn't imagine how they were able to get this rice into the thick jungle. Each bag looked as if it weighed about five hundred pounds, something that needed to be loaded onto a truck with a hi-lo. However, there were no roads, no vehicles, just small trails through thick underbrush. These people had tremendous endurance and were living in unbearable situations. The South Vietnamese soldiers could not compare with or defeat such a force of determination and shrewdness as the Vietcong.

That night we stayed within the enemy compound. Alongside our A-Cav lay a dead VC. On guard duty that evening I could not take my eyes off of him, lying there with ants and flies covering him. The smell of death was everywhere. The napalm that was dropped from the jet fighters had scorched the jungle floor. The stench of burning flesh was hard to bear, and to this day I cannot erase it from my mind. The sergeant of the lead tank of our squad did not make it. He died on the helicopter, but the young man he rescued survived. The next day we pushed forward looking for more enemy positions, the thoughts of home like a dream, a place of nonexistence.

Back at camp (I have the hat on)

Uncovering a mine

Back from patrol - I am in the middle

Chapter 14

I lost track of time, the day of the week and the month. It was surreal, a world of madness, an endless cycle of insanity. After months in the field, we finally returned back to base camp. I was glad to be able to sleep in a cot instead of on the ground. Back at camp was a time of mischievous pranks and smoking marijuana in our private hideout. It didn't last long, though.

Early one morning I was called out, along with a few others, to the captain's office. We soon found out that we had been volunteered to mine-sweep for the second squadron, somewhere near the Cambodian border. I do not know why I was chosen, probably because of my rebellious attitude back in camp, but I did not want to go.

It was hard to ride with others that we had not been with in battle. We were flown out on choppers and dropped off in the middle of a jungle clearing. The second squadron picked us up after the helicopters flew away, and we had to ride with the artillery on top of the ammo carrier. The second squadron had just received a new captain. He was a hardball. He ordered the men to ride partially inside the tanks and A-Cavs. This was not smart. Most of us rode on top with our legs folded under us. Riding with your legs inside was dangerous, because when the RPG's would hit a tank or an A-Cav, they would explode inside, tearing off your legs. If we rode on top and it was hit, chances were we would be blown off the track, without losing a limb. This man refused to let his men ride on top, however, and I sensed we were in trouble from the start.

Not long into the jungles, we were ambushed. RPG's and small arms fire were fired at us. The first tank that was hit was the captain's. He lost his legs, and was flown out on the chopper. I do not know if he survived, but I think not.

There seemed to be mass confusion among us. With the captain gone and the enemy hitting us so quickly, we were left stunned. Evening came on us like a dark shadow. Not far from where we were ambushed, we set up in a wagon train circle, but because of the confusion, no one put out trip flares or barbed wire. The artillery was in the middle; the rounds were tossed on the ground and were armed. There seemed to be no one in charge.

A friend and I got together and started smoking pot. One of the soldiers from the other outfit rebuked us, and said, "You shouldn't be smoking that garbage out here." We just shrugged it off and continued. I was stoned when I crawled under one of the Howitzer guns. It was a 155-artillery track, and weighed over sixty tons. I figured it was a safe place to sleep for the night, and I quickly fell asleep, my mind in a daze from the pot I had smoked.

The flash of an explosion suddenly awakened me. All around us was fire. An RPG hit the track I was under. Another explosion, and I knew we were hit again. The artillery rounds on the ground were in the midst of the flames, and we knew we had to get away from where we were. One of the men took off; I could not follow because I could not locate my rifle. My mind still in a daze from the pot, I was filled with confusion. I crawled away without a weapon.

Bullets where zinging through the air, more RPG's struck their targets. There seemed to be nothing that was not on fire. I made my way to the command track in the center of the compound. The officers were filled with as much confusion as I was. I didn't want to be too close to their track because I feared that it would be the next to get hit by an RPG. One young man handed me a weapon and I crawled off. I found a B52 bomb crater where some other troops had gathered, and we all kept low, as the artillery within the compound started to explode. Not only were we being attacked from without, the danger from within was worse. Shrapnel flew everywhere. We put out a field of fire in front of us, hoping to keep from getting a ground attack. I believe the enemy would have attacked us, had not the explosions from our own artillery held them back. It was a night of terror, as though we were in the center of hell. I could see tanks silhouetted in the night smoking from the RPG hits they had taken. We were totally caught off guard.

It was a long night. By early morning we were still huddled within the bomb crater. Piles of ash and metal were strewn across the jungle floor. Within the center of the compound, clouds of smoke hovered over twisted metal like a dark shadow. The damage was horrendous. It seemed as though every armored vehicle had been hit. Men were crying out in pain from their wounds, others lay dead.

The Medic helicopters arrived, and gun ships flew above, searching the jungle for snipers or any enemy position that might still be near our position. We helped carry the dead and wounded to the choppers. There were so many that it was hard to comprehend all that had happened.

I looked for the Howitzer I slept under, but all that was left was the base of it. Nothing else remained. This sixty-ton vehicle was gone, along with its barrel and tracks. I had thought that nothing could do so much damage. The artillery that was within its big gun had exploded; the barrel was found hundreds of yards away. I wondered what had happened to the sergeant that slept inside the Howitzer. I didn't have to wait long to find out. I was helping load a pile of ash, and after placing it on a rain poncho, we each held a corner and ran to the chopper. I looked down at the pile, not knowing what it was, until I saw a piece of paper tagged to the poncho with the sergeant's name on it.

I thought about being under that big gun the night of the attack and how secure I felt. I realized then that I could not hide from death. It was a day of despair and tragedy. Many mistakes were made that cost the lives of these young men. I located the men from our outfit, and each shared his own story of the attack.

The tanks that could still move headed out; I was on an A-Cav because the ammo carrier that I came with was gone. We hooked up with another outfit and kept going deeper into the jungle.

The next night was a night that no one slept. I found another bomb crater along our perimeter, and set up watch there along with some other men. That night we put out our trip flares and barbed wire, and held a tight watch. My mind whirled with thoughts of the previous night, the explosions, panic and chaos were like a nagging nightmare. It was ever before me. I was fearful thinking that it would happen again, but the night was quiet and by morning we traveled on.

Chapter 15

It was Thanksgiving Day, 1969, and we found a clearing in which to set up camp. Choppers flew in some hot food for us in remembrance of the holiday. There was not much to celebrate; I could not help but think of the sergeant, his poncho, and his remains. It was seared into my conscience.

I was tired mentally, physically, and spiritually. I had no peace. I thought of death often, wondering what came after this life. I tried to convince myself that we just die and that's it. Nonetheless, the thought of judgment, of a place where I would have to answer for my sins, haunted me day in and day out. I tried to deny the existence of God, but I could not. Even in the midst of such hatred, pain and death, something continually whispered to my heart that there was a peace that I had never known. I so longed for peace. I wanted to know happiness, but it seemed like only a fleeting hope in my life, something for others to have, but always out of my grasp.

We traveled on, searching and destroying anything and everything we found that belonged to the enemy. I was flown out of the jungle because of a tooth infection; this gave me a brief time of relief from the jungles. A friend and I took advantage of this time and headed into Saigon. Combat troops were not allowed in Saigon, so we had to be careful not to get caught. Saigon was a city caught up in the craze of the war. There was a lot of selling of black-marketed products. Things that were to be used by military only found their way into the marketplace.

We stayed a few days and partied, and then knew we had to return. I picked up the mailbag to take out with us; I knew the troops in the field really looked forward to the mail. We caught a helicopter ride out to our position.

I remember there was a young man traveling with us. He was new, and was heading for his company post. He had not yet seen battle, however, when we were dropped off in the jungle, we were in the midst of a major battle. As the helicopter was descending, a jet fighter was dropping napalm not far from our position. On the ground we could see men firing their weapons as the helicopter touched down. Men carrying wounded ran to our chopper so they could load them on. I remember the young man that was on the chopper crying, saying that he was not supposed to be there. I just shrugged him off, jumped out, and ran toward our troops. Even though bullets where zinging through the air like a disturbed bunch of bees, the men in our outfit were more concerned about the mail. They were relieved to see me running with the bag over my shoulder, and in the midst of all the havoc I was yelling out, with a smile on my face, "I got the mail! I got the mail!"

Back at base camp, things were changing. Most of the men I knew were gone, and new replacements had come in. I never felt at ease with the change. It didn't seem that I could get close to anybody again. More and more I was becoming a recluse. Smoking pot seemed to numb the pain within, but each night I was still haunted by all that was happening.

We were sent out again into the jungle. We were on patrol near the Cambodian border, traveling alongside some rice patties, when a captain from another outfit chose a few of us to follow him on the ground. We headed into the rice patties, away from the A-Cav's. We were walking through the flooded patties, and the heat made it difficult to wear the jackets that protected us from shrapnel. I was so hot that I took my jacket off, and trudged along behind the captain. I wasn't sure what he was doing or where he was taking us. As we were walking, I noticed something off in the brush on the edge of the jungle that bordered the river. It looked like a boat. I informed the captain, and we cautiously headed in that direction. It was a VC boat hidden away, probably used for carrying weapons and men. As we searched the area for more signs, the crack of an AK-47 shattered the silence. There was a sniper across the river from us. He was not shooting at us, but at a helicopter gun-ship that was overhead. The gunner on the helicopter quickly responded back with a burst of machine-gun fire. He saw us in the bush then, and thought we were the enemy – the bullets spattered at our feet, dust flew up, and zinging sounds of flying shells seemed to rip right by us. Fortunately there was a large dugout hole that we quickly jumped into. The captain quickly radioed ahead and told them that we were American troops. He was so angry that I thought he was going to have one of the tanks shoot the helicopter down. I just wanted out, the sweat rolled down my face like a rainfall, and each drop was a disdainful reminder of what a hellhole this place was.

The next time I went out I was on a lead track and it was Christmas morning. I was watching the minesweepers in front of us who were trying to clear the path before us. They were all new, and I wondered if they knew what they were doing. One young man I met had just arrived in the country and they sent him out right away. He told me he was recently married; I think he was only eighteen or nineteen years old. He was one of the sweepers I was watching. Suddenly one of the men bent over to probe the ground, when a burst of machine-gun fire shattered the silence of that early Christmas morning. The young man who was just newly wed and new in the country lay dead on the ground. Everyone started shooting into the jungles, thinking a sniper had hit us, but I knew what had happened. The man who had bent over to check for the mine had two M16 rifles – each one strapped to a shoulder. Instead of giving them to someone to hold, he just kept them strapped to him as he probed the ground. One of the safeties was not on, and when he bent over, something on his belt set off the trigger, causing a burst of bullets to be released. The young man I had met was directly in front of him, with his back facing the man with the M16's. This young boy, just married, never knew what hit him. They reported it as sniper fire, and later on they even promoted the man who shot him. That day I thought about his young wife and Christmas; there would be no joy for her or for his mother or father. I was grieved for them, and wanted to escape.

Chapter 16

In late March, early April, 1970, my time in Vietnam was getting close to its end. I didn't want to go out into the jungles anymore. Only weeks left, with over two years in this war behind me. I wanted to go home, I wanted to live. I continued to be sent out because they said I was a good mine-sweeper, but back at base camp I was nothing but trouble. I was a specialist E-5, the same rank as a staff sergeant, and I used this rank to keep myself out of a lot of duties. I hated being in camp, but I didn't want to be out in the field, either. I just wanted it all to end. Whenever I was flown out to the jungles for action, I would bring at least a pound of pot with me. It was a standard practice among the troops who hung together and smoked.

I had only about ten days left when I was told that I had to go back in the field. I protested, but was commanded to go and get my equipment. Resentfully, I returned to my tent, and started filling my duffel bag. I found a pound of marijuana where I had stashed it under some sand bags, and put it into my bag. Just about the time I hid the weed, a young sergeant about my age stuck his head into my tent and said, "they're going to try to bust you," and then he left. I quickly went through my bags, took out the pot, and hid it where it could not be found. I reported to the command post. They told me to come inside with my bags.

The new captain was not too fond of me, or of some of the other seasoned veterans. He told me to empty my bags on his desk, so I did, knowing that I had nothing to hide. I asked him if he wanted to check my underwear, and I held up a dirty pair. I was angry and sarcastic, knowing what they were trying to do. I had spent over two years in the war, and now I was being tricked into something. They wanted my rank to be taken away. I did not see the error of my ways, because I felt, along with others, that everybody in this war was in error. They did not find what they were looking for, so they sent me out to the field, even though I had only ten days left.

I reluctantly boarded the chopper and was flown out to the position. I mine-swept some roads, cleared some mines out, and then requested to return to camp. Because of my short time I was allowed to return to base camp. I said good-bye to those of the men I had known, and I boarded the chopper. As we flew back, I took my last look at the jungles; this country had been my home for over two years. Though I was glad to be leaving, there was sadness within. The thoughts of those I had known, and those left behind reminded me of how frail life is, and I wondered what was ahead for me.

Back at base camp I packed my things and prepared to leave. I took a plane to Bien Hoa where I waited for "the freedom bird," a name we had given the plane that would take us home. It was early morning when we were taken to the airstrip, the same airstrip where I had arrived more than two years prior. I thought of the night I first came, and of the man who told me to forget everything I had learned.

It was a quiet morning – birds were just starting to sing, as if there were no war going on. I landed in Vietnam in the midst of utter chaos; I was leaving in quiet serenity. It was hard to believe I was going home, that I had made it out alive.

Chapter 17

The sun was rising; it looked as if it was coming right out of the end of the airstrip. It was a beautiful sunrise, a deep reddish-orange. I couldn't remember ever seeing the sun look so big as it broke forth, awakening this new day. The freedom bird was coming. I watched as it landed, descending right in central view of the sunrise. It was a morning I will never forget.

We boarded the plane, about two hundred of us. Thoughts of a rocket or mortar hitting the plane entered my mind, and I could not wait until the plane was airborne. The flight was long, about twenty-four hours. It was April 29th, 1970. I was going home.

We landed in New York. At the airport we had to wait for about six hours for buses from Fort Dix, New Jersey, to come and pick us up. The people at the airport were cold to us, and passengers ignored us, as though we were not there. I wondered if it was like this for other troops who had returned home. There were no welcomes, no pats on the back, no thanks, just looks of disapproval. I didn't care. I just wanted out of my military clothing and into some civilians. I was going to be discharged. My days of Army life were now over, and a whole life was now in front of me.

The buses came and took us on a long ride to Fort Dix. At Dix we had to be initiated back into the system. They ran us through a series of medical tests, asked all kinds of questions to make sure we had not gone insane from the effects of the war. I was sarcastic as usual. I just wanted my papers and pay so I could leave. Finally they took our jungle fatigues, and gave us brand new military dress uniforms. They sewed our rank and regiment patch on our uniforms. I dressed in mine, but knew as soon as I was back at the barracks I would take it off and throw it away. My name was called, they issued my papers and pay, then saluted me, and said I could go.

Three years had passed; three years that drastically changed my life. I had seen the worst that men could do, and I was now a veteran, something to be proud of, so they told us. However, I did not feel any honor. I felt awkward, out of place, a stranger in a strange land.

On my way back to the barracks, I ripped off my tie, opened my shirt buttons, and carried my dress jacket over my shoulder. A colonel saw me and jumped out of his vehicle, came over to me and started rebuking me for looking the way I did. I let him finish, and then told him I was just honorably discharged. It didn't matter to him; he thought I was out of place with my attitude, and I was. The uniform that I had once proudly worn stood for the freedom of our country. Many lives had been lost by those who had worn it and by those who had fought to keep our country free. Be that as it may, all I could think about was being out. The Vietnam Veterans were not honored, but mocked and criticized by many in our country. Even the press did not respect us, so I did not want any association with what I had just lived through. Back at the barracks, I quickly undressed, put my civilian clothes on, went outside and put my uniform in the trash.

I left Fort Dix with another young veteran that I had met on the plane. We took a bus to Manhattan, and decided we would stay a few days and party. We went to Greenwich Village where all the hippies hung out. We checked into a cheap room, and then walked the streets.

All the lights, nightclubs, and excitement were so different. We went to a place where a band was playing. Everyone had long hair. Black lights, glowing posters, and the smell of pot permeated the air. We tried to fit in, but our short hair and clothing made us stick out like a sore thumb. No one would talk to us, and we soon realized that we were not welcome. I kept thinking that this was supposed to be the generation of peace and love. I felt neither. We looked up one family that my friend knew in New York; we stayed awhile with them and partied. After smoking pot and drinking, we went back to the room. My first night back in the States left me cold within. My expectations were shattered. I felt so alone and out of sorts.

After a few days, I decided to fly back home. I had my fill of New York City. I arrived in Detroit, Michigan, about 10 a.m. in the morning. No one was there to greet me. I don't remember if I told anyone I was coming home. I had to take a taxi the twenty-five miles to my home. I remember the taxi driver, a young black man, who seemed interested in my Vietnam experience. He was the only friendly person I had met since I returned. I enjoyed my ride with him and gave him a big tip when he dropped me off at home.

Chapter 18

I had missed our big house on the shore of Lake Erie. I loved being by the water. The fresh scent of the breeze that blew across the lake greeted me, and it felt so good to be home. My mother was surprised to see me. She hugged me and wanted to cook me something to eat. I unpacked my things, and was ready to go find some old friends.

I had sent money home while in Vietnam, so that I could purchase a car. My mom and my step-dad Tom had purchased a Pontiac convertible. It was a beauty. I was soon out riding in it, with the top down, even though it was still chilly. I didn't want to think about the war. It was over for me, something in my past. However the memories haunted me each night.

I soon found a job in a small plant that manufactured car batteries. Each day after work I would get high. Everyone in the factory was much older than I. One man in particular had ten children, and he worked very hard to support them. I knew it had to be hard on him working in a small plant like this. I was filled with anxiety. I didn't want to end up spending the rest of my life working in a place such as this, so I quit.

I decided to hitchhike to Florida with a friend of mine. We only made it to Kentucky and came back. I found another job, at a Ford plant, and decided I would move out. I found a motel room that rented monthly.

The day I moved in I met my neighbor. We had to share the same bathroom, as our rooms were connected. I soon found out that this guy was selling drugs. I didn't know much about heroin, only that some soldiers in Vietnam were hooked on it. This man was selling it. I had no desire to touch it; however, one of my friends was coaxed into trying some. I watched him stick a needle in his arm for the first time. He was addicted not long after.

My life soon took a downward swing. I was laid-off, and found myself with a lot of time on my hands. It was summer, and going to the beach was common for us.

One day we met a man who wanted to buy some drugs. I didn't want anything to do with the guy, yet he persisted, and one of my friends said he would bring some the next day. I didn't think much about it, because I had no dealings with this man. However, the next day we did go to the beach, hours after the meeting was set. I didn't think the guy would be there, but sure enough, he was. When we pulled in he pursued us; I suspected him of being an undercover policeman, and tried to avoid him. We tested him by asking him to smoke pot with us. He agreed. However, when we tried to light up, a patrol car came through the park. I jumped into the man's vehicle, as he asked me to get in with him. I was nervous, and knew something was wrong. He kept telling me how close of a call that was, and that he was glad we didn't get busted.

I had some drugs hidden on me, and he pestered me to see them. I pulled them out, and quickly he started counting money, throwing it in my lap as he finished counting each bill. He was bugged, and as soon as he said "five," the police ran toward us and arrested me. It all happened so fast. The officers were all dressed in plain clothes, and were sitting at different places in the park. I was in shock. I didn't try to sell any drugs, but they told me this was what I was being arrested for. The police handcuffed me and took me to jail.

That night in the cell, I lay awake going over all that had happened. I could not believe that I was in such a bad situation. When I went to court they gave me a court-appointed lawyer, because I could not afford my own. The trial was set and I was released on bond.

I moved back home and tried to find work. I also enrolled in college. I wanted to be cleared. I did not want to spend any more time in jail.

After a few weeks, I was called down to another Ford plant. I had to take a physical to be accepted. The physical was set for early the next morning, so I decided to stay at the same motel where my friend was still living because it was closer to the clinic. I was watching TV in the motel room that night about 9:00 p.m. when my friend returned with a bag of drugs. I didn't know that drugs were being delivered to the room that evening, but soon after, people began to show up, wanting to buy drugs. I began to feel nervous and wanted to get out, but before I knew it, the police were kicking in the door.

Here I was, arrested again for selling drugs. My chance for school and the job were shattered. This time I was in the jail cell with about seven people who were all arrested in the room. Each of us appeared before the judge, and each was released on bond, except me, because I already had a case pending.

Off to the county jail I was sent, to await my court dates. I knew things were worse then ever because of the second bust. It didn't matter that the drugs were not mine. I was in the room, and considered as guilty as the rest. I was finally released on bond after about sixty days of waiting in the county jail.

My life was now more confused than ever. I tried to get myself in order. I looked for a job and enrolled in another school. The state-appointed lawyer never had much time for me. I was just a pick of the draw for him.

The day of my court date came. I dressed up in a suit, and was there early. When my name was called I stood before the judge with my lawyer. The lawyer was asked if he had anything to say for me, and he responded, "No, your honor." Then the judged turned to me. I do not remember much of what he said, because of the fear that overwhelmed me. I was sentenced to two to ten years in prison. Never a word was said about my military past, or my efforts to change. I could not believe that I was going to prison. I had not been out of the war but a short time, and now I was going to be incarcerated.

I didn't want to live anymore; my heart was crushed from all that I had gone through. I knew I was wrong for having drugs in the first place, and understood that I deserved what I was getting. However, the thought of being in prison was hard to bear.

I was sent to three different institutions. The last one was where I spent most of my time. I went to school there, and worked hard at it. My favorite place to go during free time was the library. I started consuming books. I was interested in reading eastern mysticism books, and I practiced Yoga daily. I became a vegetarian, and wouldn't even eat eggs.

At night I would meditate in my cell for hours, trying to reach a higher state of consciousness. I felt a sense of power; that I had found something that I could relate to. However, there was still within me a sense of the guilt of sin. I thought I could overcome this in time with the practice of meditation.

One day I read a book written by some Guru from India. About halfway through the book, I began reading a chapter about Christ. This man mocked the cross, and the blood of Christ. I found myself appalled. I quickly discarded the book, and a sense of fear came over me. I started to question the things I was getting into. I knew inside that I was clinging to a false peace; that something was wrong.

I spent my time in prison doing the right things, so I was released early. I had served fourteen months of my sentence at the time of my release. I spent my twenty-first birthday in prison, and I vowed that I would never spend another birthday behind bars. I was so glad to be free again. I felt healthy from my vegetarian diet and the yoga, and I thought I could face any problem.

I was not out of prison eight hours, however, before I was with my brothers getting high. I found a lawn care job, enrolled in the community college, and tried to do things right. Within I was still discontent; I didn't like the system, and I became a dropout as so many others. Though I worked at jobs, I thought the hippie culture had more going for it than the hypocrisy that I saw all around me. I was so restless inside that I took to the road again. I traveled to Florida, out west, and to the coast of California. There was a void within that I wanted filled, but nothing satisfied.

I was in a relationship that was on and off. I had nothing to offer, and there was no reason for anybody to want to stay with me. The relationship finally broke, and I found myself abandoned and crushed again. I had been living in California when we split up, and I traveled back home to Michigan, broken and filled with despair. Bitterness started to set in, and I lost the desire to care for others. I started carrying a gun, and started associating with some of my old friends who were involved with hard drugs. I even met a policeman who sold guns to anybody who wanted one.

One night I was at a party with some friends. There were a lot of drugs being passed around, which made me nervous. One man came and brought a new person to the party. Right away I felt uneasy. I did not want to go to jail again. This man looked to me like an undercover cop. He had long hair, which looked like a wig, and he was wearing a bandana. I was sitting on the floor by a big pillow. I had a gun in my pants, a small .22 pistol. I watched this man, every move he made. Suddenly he went into the bathroom and closed the door. I became suspicious and very nervous. It was as though a voice was telling me that the man was a cop, and that when he came out of the bathroom, he would have a pistol drawn and would arrest everyone. I was facing the bathroom; I pulled my pistol out and kept it at my side as I sat on the floor. I didn't know what I would do if he came out with a gun. All I knew was that I was scared, and did not want to go back to jail. The bathroom door opened; I had my finger on the trigger, with the gun hidden at my side. He came out, but with no pistol. I quickly got up and left the party. I was shaking from the experience. I wondered what I would have done, and the thought of shooting him scared me. I don't think that I would have, but the thought of it troubled me for days on end.

Months later I was staying in a small shack out in the country with a friend. One night, I wrote in a little journal that I had tried to keep. In it I told myself that I had to leave, and not return until my life was changed. I was lost, bewildered, confused and burdened with my sinful heart. I didn't want to be this way. I truly wanted a change, but everything I tried to do right had failed. There was such a weight of condemnation on my shoulders, a burden that was hard to bear. I stood in that shack wondering what I should do. At the same time, the words of a Bob Dylan song that was playing on the stereo pierced my heart like an arrow: "Leave your stepping stones behind, something calls for you. Forget the dead you left, they will not follow you. The vagabond is rapping at your door, is standing in the clothes that you once wore; strike another match, go start anew, and it's all over now, baby blue."

I wanted to start anew – to escape from the vagabond that I had become. I decided that night that I would leave to search for truth, or die trying.

Chapter 19

Within a few days I was packed; I had only a backpack and a journal to take with me, and my dog Nature. My friend Pat (whom I had known for years) had a van, and we were going to travel together. The night we left I was in my brother's apartment. He had some books on a shelf, and I asked him if I could take one. I chose one book in particular because of the picture on its cover. It had a backpacker on the front – he was heading off in the direction of a light. I felt like I belonged in this picture. I had no idea what the book was about, but the picture and its title seemed to draw me to it. The title of the book was: *Pilgrim's Progress.*

We headed out toward Florida. Our objective was to go to the Mardi-Gras in New Orleans. I had never been there, and had heard so much about it. I could not shake the words of Bob Dylan. I felt I was striking another match, a new flame – a change was ahead. Nonetheless, the burden of sin weighed heavily on my heart. I started to read the book on the way to Florida. The first chapter was intriguing. The man's backpack I soon found out was the weight of his sin. The book was an allegory of a man looking for truth. I felt so much like the pilgrim in the book. I was carrying the same burden; the weight of the sin I could not escape. All that I had done continued to burden me. The more I tried to cover it up with the pleasures of this life, the more it tormented me.

We stopped in Jacksonville, Florida. There I spent time on the beach reading *Pilgrim's Progress.*

Each sentence, each chapter spoke to my heart. I felt I was living this book. The same despair this man had, I had. I did not want to be a part of the world I was in. I knew that I, too, was lost in sin, and that judgment awaited me. Was there any hope? All the religions that I had tried were irreparable and without answers. All the pleasures that I tried to fill my life with left me feeling empty. I was still in a prison, one that had no key. I was a prisoner of sin; there was a spiritual vacuum within that I could not fill no matter how I tried. I felt captive in a world full of darkness and despair.

In Florida we traveled from city to city with no real direction. Like the wind, we seemed to blow every which way. We landed a short-term job at Ringling Brothers circus in concessions. This gave us some finances with which to travel. When the circus relocated, we followed. Soon we grew tired of this and decided to head to New Orleans. The day before we left, the van broke down. Our only choice was to hitchhike, the two of us with our two dogs and our backpacks.

We traveled across interstate I-10 that took us west. Getting rides was difficult, but somehow we managed. We arrived in New Orleans right before the Mardi-Gras started. People were coming from all over the country. This was the party place of the year, where rich and poor alike came to take in the festivities.

It didn't feel like much of a celebration to me. I was feeling more and more alienated from all that I was seeing. I was tired of being hungry and struggling to even find a place to lay my head. We found an abandoned house where we decided we could sleep, but soon found out that we were not the only ones with the same idea. When evening came the house was filled. Every corner seemed to have a body lying in it. There were drunks, hippies, and street hustlers. I was thankful for the dogs; nobody seemed to bother us with the two large canines always at our side. My dog, Nature, was my closest companion; she seemed to know the burden I carried within. At night she would crawl into my sleeping bag and sleep at the bottom of my feet. She always nudged me when I seemed down, and at times I felt she was encouraging me to keep going, as if to say that there was something ahead, if I would just not give up. She was never far from my side. If I were in a shop or restaurant, she would lay outside the building by my backpack, untied. If anyone came near my things, Nature would just raise her lip, show her teeth, and that was all that was needed to keep strangers away. I look back now, and I know that God crossed my path with this Golden Labrador. He knew what I needed even before I could understand anything. Even as a pup, she would sleep on my forehead. That animal was more of a friend than I had ever known. She was the added edge I needed to see that there was a Creator that cared. As each day passed, I was drawn to the things of creation, and I abhorred the inventions of man.

My stomach sickened from the sights we saw as we walked the streets of the Mardi-Gras. People were drunk, high, and the lusts of the flesh filled the streets. It seemed as if there were no moral restraint; a modern-day Sodom and Gomorrah.

The only enjoyment I found was going to the park and sitting under a tree in the warm sun, reading *Pilgrim's Progress*. I loved watching the sun rise, and the sounds of early morning, with all manner of birds singing their tunes. Life seemed to be exploding into abundant joy all around me. Each day started with this same wondrous show, but people were missing it. It was as though God was shouting to us with a love beyond measure, yet we seemed to be deaf and blind to His marvelous truth.

My heart was softening with each day. I felt a driving force within, something compelling me to press on and to look up, as if to say that my redemption was near. I had no desire to party; I had no more longings for the things of this life. I was being stripped of all that seemed to chain me to a life of utter despondency.

One night I was out in the streets alone. It was about four in the morning. I remember standing against a police barricade that was used to keep cars from entering the French quarter, the place where the festivities were being held. At first there was not a soul around. Everyone was asleep or passed out from the celebration. Then I noticed down the main street a party of people walking toward me. I could tell that they had come from some kind of expensive engagement. Some were dressed in tuxedoes, others in highly fashioned gowns. I thought at first that it was a wedding party, until they drew closer. I soon found out that they were all men – men dressed as women, holding hands and kissing each other. My stomach sickened.

I went back to the abandoned house and just laid there, awake, realizing what an awful place I had found myself in. This party of parties became a living hell to me. I lay on my sleeping bag as roaches scurried across the floor, but they did not seem to be anywhere near as disgusting as what I had seen that night.

The next morning I went to the park and sat under the tree I had visited each day. I was reading in *Pilgrim's Progress* a chapter that told the story about Christian and his friend Faithful traveling to a town called Vanity Fair. In Vanity Fair people tried to sell them their goods. Women tried to entice them, but Christian and his friend would have no part of it. Instead, Faithful made a stand and told the people they needed truth, and to flee from the judgment to come. Christian and Faithful where arrested, thrown into jail, and were taken to court. They found Faithful guilty of a crime. His only crime was speaking the truth. They flogged Christian and sent him from the town. They burned Faithful at the stake. However, the Lord was there to greet Faithful at the end of his journey and to award him the crown of life.

I was fascinated with what I was reading. Everything I was seeing at this celebration was like Vanity Fair. I thought to myself, "What would happen if a person like Faithful stood up and proclaimed the truth at this Mardi-Gras? Would he be arrested?" What burdened my heart about this part of the story was that Christian and Faithful knew to Whom they belonged; they would have no place among those who refused the truth.

As for me, at that moment I knew I was a part of the world around me. I did not have what these two pilgrims had. I wanted to flee this dark place; to escape from a judgment that I knew would one day come upon this world of greed and sin.

As I sat there thinking on these things, a policeman came up and told me to move. I couldn't understand why. This was a park and I was just sitting and reading, not bothering anybody. He became angry when I questioned him, and told me I was killing the grass. I knew that if I pressed the issue any further, I would be arrested. My hair was long and I was considered part of the "undesirables," those who had little money to spend. I found out that a lot of people like me, the "hitchhikers" or "hippies," as we were labeled, were arrested and put to work on a farm until the Mardi-Gras was over. The law had no tolerance for vagrants or vagabonds. If you had money to spend they cared less how you acted, but those like me were singled out and removed.

I found Pat and told him that I wanted to leave, that I was sick of this place. Within hours we were back on the freeway, hitchhiking toward Texas.

My good friend "Nature"

Chapter 20

My mother had moved to Texas because of Tom's work. I knew that my mom's house was a place I could go to where I would not be turned away. It took us but a few days to arrive in Texas. Our last ride was from a man who was drunk. His driving was terrible, and I wondered if we would get there alive.

On the way there, I somehow acquired a "Good News For Modern Man," the New Testament written in modern English. I was finishing *Pilgrim's Progress*, reading about Christian's final journey and his joyful entrance into the celestial city, and I desperately wanted to believe in what I was reading. I hungered for God, but I felt my sins had sealed my fate. I read how Christian had lost his burden and sin at the foot of the cross. Was it real, or all a wishful dream? Was there a God who had me on His mind? Was there such a place for a man like me to be washed clean? My life was full of disappointments; my hopes were always shattered. I was scared to even believe that these things could be true. I could not take another disappointment. I had guarded my heart and locked it into a prison of insecurities. I did not want anybody to get too close to me, because I knew that sooner or later, I would be crushed within my spirit. I was scared – truly scared.

Each night I wept, wanting to believe, but fearing that it was just a fantasy, something beyond my reach. I was so dry within, but my soul thirsted for truth. Something deep within me kept softly speaking to my heart, that there was an answer; a hope that I had never known. I kept thinking about the cross and He who died on it, and I asked myself, "Why?" I had seen so much of what was called Christianity, and it soured my stomach. I wondered, "Is there something more real than what I have seen?" I had reached out to those who confessed His name, yet they had turned their backs on me in my greatest need. I wondered if there was a belief greater than this.

I started to read the New Testament that I had acquired, starting with the gospel of Matthew. Something strange happened as I read the first chapter. In the past, I had glanced through the Bible, but nothing made much sense. However, this time it seemed to be alive, and I consumed each word with an unexplainable desire and energy that I had never known before. It was as though I were at the birth of Christ as Matthew recorded the account. I could almost hear the angels proclaim to the shepherds the wonderful news of the birth of the Savior.

While at my mother's, I was able to find a job, but each day at work I could not wait to get home to read more of the Scriptures. There was no other world for me but the book that so came alive to me. Reading the accounts of the crucifixion was almost too hard for me to bear. I could see the nails being driven in by the Roman soldiers. It was as though I could feel the crown of thorns as it was mockingly placed upon His head. Each account of the trial and mistreatment of the Lord pierced my heart with the reality that truly Christ gave His life for sinful man. When they gambled for His clothes, and the people mocked him as He shed His blood, I could see myself among the crowd, and I cried knowing that my years had been spent mocking Him, rejecting Him, and living my life in selfishness and sin.

On March 18, 1976, I was alone in the apartment. I remember it was almost midnight. I was reading the gospel of John, the third chapter. I came to the verses: "For God so loved the world, that He gave His only begotten Son, that whoever believes in Him should not perish, but have eternal life. For God did not send the Son into the world to judge the world, but that the world should be saved through Him." I fell to my knees in utter shame and humility. I knew I was a wicked young man before a holy and awesome God, a sinner in need of mercy. I believed, I truly believed. Tears poured down my face as I cried out for His forgiveness. All the years of darkness, all the pains and burdens I carried, all the hate, bitterness and despair I felt released from my life. The room seemed to be filled with a light beyond anything I had ever known. A love I had never felt before, or could ever imagine to be real swept through my heart, and I knew I was truly born again; that He, who shed His blood for me, had washed me clean.

The tears of sorrow were now replaced with a joy unspeakable. I knew; I really, really knew that I was saved by His grace. I wanted to shout, with all that was in me, that I was free. I was so excited. I felt as though I were floating on air, as if heaven had come to me – and it had. I did not know much of all that I had read except that amazing grace had saved a wretch like me. I ran into the bathroom and filled the sink with water and baptized myself. I did not even know why I was doing this, except that I knew His blood washed me clean, and as I poured the water over myself, I truly felt His cleansing power. I was once lost, but was now found; blind, but now I could see.

I could not understand how I could have missed it for so long. I wondered why no one had shared such good news with me. Then I thought of Private Johnson, his smile that lit up his face like a light bulb, and his love for Jesus. I understood his joy, for now it dwelled in me. I wanted to tell everybody. All the prisons that held me captive within now unlocked, and like an eagle that soars the skies, my heart experienced a depth and height I never knew existed. All the fears now released, all the sorrows and pains that had ripped me apart now healed by the stripes of Christ my King. Even as I write this I remember the moment as if it were today. Even more so because years have passed since that wondrous night and His promise remains true. He has never left or forsaken me.

Chapter 21

With each new day my heart seemed to leap with joy. I was engrossed in the Word. I could not get enough of it. I found a Christian bookstore, and picked up some reading material to add to my ever-increasing desire to know more of the kingdom of God.

As the days passed, I found myself wanting to return to Michigan, so I saved enough money to buy a used car and planned the day to leave. I was so thankful for my time in Texas; it was the place I came to know the Lord. I always think back on how the Lord humbled me in Humble, Texas. It was a good place to be saved, in my mother's home. I so appreciated her and Tom and all they had done for me. They opened the door for me in a time of my greatest need; and I opened the door of my heart to the Lord who met those needs beyond all that I could have ever hoped for.

The trip back to Michigan was one of excitement and anxious anticipation. When I left Michigan, I left many things undone. My life was ruined, and I was on my way to hell. Now I was a new man, born again, and I wondered where the Lord would take me. I knew there was some warrants out for my arrest, because there were some traffic violations that I hadn't taken care of. On my way I prayed that the Lord would help me clear up these matters. I knew I didn't have any money to pay the tickets. I didn't even have a place to stay when I arrived. However, the Lord knows how to handle things for us.

When I arrived in Michigan I stopped at my brother's house. I left my dog there so she would be able to run instead of being cooped up in the car, and I drove around, wondering what to do about a job and a place to live. This was my first trial as a Christian. I could not get the thought of the tickets out of my mind. I felt I should turn myself in, but I reasoned with myself that I didn't have any money. I could almost hear the Lord say, "Why don't you trust Me?" but I thought it would be better to wait until I had the money to pay for the fines before I turned myself in. Be that as it may, the Lord had other plans.

It seemed no sooner had I reasoned these things out, when I heard a siren behind me. I looked in my mirror and saw a police car. I was being pulled over. The next thing I knew I was handcuffed and taken to jail. I had no idea that I had so many unpaid tickets. I found out that about three cities had citations for me. Here I was a new man, a Christian being thrown into jail.

All of my belongings were taken from me, but I was allowed to keep my Bible. It was a paperback entitled: "The Way." I was put into a holding cell my first night. There were about ten people all crowded in the same cell. I grabbed a blanket and found a corner to sit in. I felt uneasy and saddened in my heart. I knew the Lord had saved me, but I couldn't understand why He would allow me to be back in jail. I never wanted to see the inside of one of these places again, but now it seemed as if nothing had changed. I was guilty of not paying the fines, but I thought I would be able to pay them off.

That night as I sat in the corner with my Bible hidden under my blanket, I found comfort in reading the Psalms. I didn't want anybody to see the Bible; it was as though I were ashamed. I did not like the feeling of hiding God's Word, but I lacked the courage to bring it out for fear of being mocked.

That same evening a young black man was watching me. He approached me and asked: "What's under the blanket?" I pulled out my Bible and then he said, "Why are you hiding it?" We began to talk. I found myself excited about sharing. Words I didn't know were there flowed from my mouth; all that I had been studying, all the Lord had been showing me came forth like living waters. A miracle was happening; this young man wanted Jesus, and we prayed. I felt as though I were in heaven, and not in a cell. I could not feel the bars. The dirt and smell seemed to be gone; just a sweet aroma filled my heart and my nostrils. I was so ashamed for hiding the Word, and now so excited for sharing it. I told myself that day that I would never hide God's Word again.

The next day in court I was told the amount of my fine and informed that if I could not pay it that I would have to spend ten days in jail. There were also the other tickets in the different cities that still needed to be taken care of. I knew I would have to stay the ten days because I didn't have any money, and that when the ten days were up, I would be transferred to another jail for another court date.

Though things seemed so dim my first months as a Christian, I felt the joy of the Lord. I told the Lord that I would stay in jail as long as it took to clear my name. Besides, I realized I had a captive audience. I wanted to share with everybody my new found faith. I thought jail would be the hardest place to talk about Jesus, among thieves, drunks, and drug addicts. However, I realized that I was just like them, and the Lord had saved me. Just as much as He loved me, He loved them; just as He died for me, He died for their sins also.

Each day I sat with someone and talked about the love of God. There was always a hungry heart more than willing to listen.

About my third day in jail, my name was called. I was told that I had a visitor. I could not imagine who had come to see me. Nobody knew that I was in jail, except for my brother. When I went to the window to see who it was, I found a friend that I had not seen in a long time. I was shocked to see him, and wondered why he would even take the time to visit me. He said just four words: "Want to get out?" I said, "Yes." He paid my fines and I was released; I was happy to be leaving, nevertheless I would miss the men that I had shared with.

Jim shook my hand and asked me if I needed a place to stay. I couldn't believe all that was happening; one minute I was in jail, the next I was out and being welcomed into someone's home. I was so thankful for Jim and for what he did. I remembered that I had other warrants and realized that the jail should have never released me with outstanding tickets. There must have been some clerical error that they missed that day, otherwise I would not have been released.

Jim took me to his home. On the way, we reminisced about old times. Then I started to share my faith with Jim. He soaked it up like a sponge. That night in his home he prayed that Jesus would come into his heart. Now I had a new friend in Christ. We both read the Word together, and our hunger seemed to intensify. It was exciting, like a great adventure. The Word of God was so alive to us.

I knew about a coffee house ministry that was about thirty miles from Jim's house. We went and visited it one Friday night. It was called "Shalom house," a place that was established by some young Christians. A movement was going on called the "Jesus movement." God's Spirit seemed to be sweeping the country, touching thousands of young lives from coast to coast. Many, like me, were hippies that had come to know Christ. Young people with such zeal; it was overwhelming. I sat in the coffee house that night, cross-legged on the floor, listening to young musicians sing songs of joy. I was so blessed; I had found so many like me who believed in Christ the King.

Jim and I returned there three times a week: Wednesday Bible studies, Friday night coffee house, and Sunday services. The distance meant nothing. The fellowship was sweet and we looked forward to each meeting. However, there was the nagging problem of the other tickets that I had yet to take care of. I seemed to reason with myself that again, when I received enough money, I would pay the fines. I would soon learn, however, that we cannot bargain with God, that He wants us to trust Him in all things, no matter the outcome.

One night I decided to camp out in my car by a little lake that I liked to swim in. Just my dog Nature and I, back in the woods, on an old two-track trail where I had parked to spend the night. That night I laid in the back seat to sleep; it was a cool summer night, and I soon dozed off thinking about the goodness of the Lord.

About four in the morning my dog began barking furiously at something at my window. I awoke to a beam of light glaring in my face. Someone outside the car was shining a flashlight at me, and yelling for me to contain my dog. I held and quieted Nature down and tried to shake off the sleep. I soon realized that it was a policeman. He had a gun pointed at me, and I had no idea why. I got out of the car and he frisked me, then he handcuffed me. I was informed that they were looking for a man who had robbed a store and then had fled into the woods. I happened to be in the area where they thought he was hiding. They quickly found that I was not the man they were looking for, but they also found that I still had a few unpaid tickets. The policeman felt bad that I was arrested for this. He knew I was just out camping. He allowed me to drive my car to my brother's house where I left my dog, and then I went with him.

On the way to jail, I knew in my heart that I had put off what God wanted me to take care of. He was trying to teach me, and I was finding out that I was a slow learner.

Back in the cellblock I found my familiar corner, and waited to be transferred to another county where I was to be arraigned. A State policeman, who just happened to be the undercover officer who had arrested me for selling drugs – the man who threw the money in my lap and set me up for the drug bust, transported me. It seemed, at first, to be a strange coincidence.

On our journey to the other county we started to talk. I told him about my new life in Christ. He was excited to hear. I told him that all things had changed, and that Christ had truly set me free. He told me that I was his first drug bust, and informed me that they were looking for me awhile back. He said that there was an undercover agent at a party who had turned in my name along with others. I realized the man he was talking about was the man to whom I had pointed my gun. He said they quit looking for me, that too much time had passed for them to find any fault with me. I could not believe all that was taking place; it was as though I were viewing some wild movie. The Lord was truly restoring the years that I had wasted.

In the cell I was able to witness to a guy who had escaped from prison. He prayed that the Lord would come into his life. His conversion was overwhelming. He seemed to light up like a light bulb. He asked me for my Bible; I told him that I would bring him one when I got out, but he insisted on having mine. I had just purchased this new Bible and found it difficult, at first, to let it go. I had marked it and worked in it; it was a part of me.

The man insisted, however, and I gave it to him. He was full of joy, and so was I.

The next day I went to court. All charges against me were dropped. I did not have to pay one fine. I was released. I was learning about trust, that God is faithful in all things. I didn't know what was ahead for me, but I knew I was to trust the Lord with all my heart, and not to lean on my own understanding, but to acknowledge Him in all things and He would make my path straight. I had learned this in the Word, now I was to learn it in my life!

One night at a Bible study a couple of young missionaries shared their stories with us. I was so intrigued by the things these men had done, and found myself longing to do the same. They told us of a short-term missions group that was going to Mexico for a Christmas outreach. I wanted to go, so I signed up. Glen, another friend from our fellowship, also signed up for the trip. We had but a few months to prepare and raise our support.

We were required to attend a prayer meeting for two weeks before we left on the trip. I remember my first night at that prayer meeting. We arrived at an old house in Detroit where the meeting was being held. When I entered the house I found a group of young people kneeling before a map of the world; a candle was lit and set in the center of the map. Each youth was on his face weeping for the lost and dying of the world. I had never experienced such devotion and compassion before. My heart felt such an urgent cry for commitment. This was a battle for souls; these young people had set their hearts toward heaven, and were willing to go wherever the Lord would lead.

I felt that evening that I had come into a part of God's kingdom that was beyond the common grounds of most churches. This was the heart of God being revealed in the souls of men. My life as a Christian would never be the same after attending that first prayer meeting.

Days passed and my heart filled with excitement in anticipation of my first short-term trip. I had purchased an old ambulance. We called it "the blue goose." I decided to drive it to Mexico instead of taking the bus, as others were going to do. I found out that if we drove, we would be asked to carry in Bibles and other supplies for the crusade. The blue goose was an ugly sight, but I was proud to have it. I wanted to do whatever God asked of me, and to go wherever He called me, and I was filled with wonder that God would use such a person like me.

My two weeks in Mexico were a time of wonder. Three hundred young people from the United States and Canada worked together with the mission organization Operation Mobilization. The director of the organization, George Verwer, was there with us, and each night as we met for prayer and fellowship, he would talk of commitment, compassion, and zeal for Christ. It was a time of spiritual growth. I learned of missionaries like Hudson Taylor, William Carey, the Judsons, Amy Carmichael, Jim Elliott, and many more who had forsaken everything for the sake of the call. I was also introduced to some wonderful writers: A. W. Tozer, Leonard Ravenhill, Charles Finney, Spurgeon, and many more. I was thankful for this source of information. It helped me understand the cross and the cost; that all we have is a gift from above, and our life is to be hidden in Christ. By grace we are saved, and only by His grace do we stand. I left Mexico with a fresh zeal in my heart, wanting to commit to missions. I was a soldier before in the United States Army; now I wanted to be a soldier for the Lord.

Chapter 22

When I arrived back home, I soon found that most Christians didn't share my interest in missions, and they looked upon me as just another wishful thinker. I applied to some mission groups but found I was not qualified, and the expense was beyond my reach as I far as I was able to see it. I became discouraged, disenchanted, and started to feel that the work of the Lord was for a special breed, for those who were more spiritual than I. I also noticed that people in the church were chosen for leadership due to their talent and popularity. I didn't understand this; I thought Christians were all the same in Christ.

I decided to leave for a while. I went to northern Michigan, where I lived in a tent for the summer. I worked doing odd jobs, picking strawberries and finding other means of making a few dollars. I was becoming discouraged. I knew I belonged to the Lord, but I had a nagging feeling that there was something I was supposed to be doing, but couldn't put my finger on it.

One morning I awoke and prayed. I decided I would just step out in faith and go south. It was early summer, 1977, when I packed my bags, my dog, and started hitchhiking to Florida. I kept thinking about Christian in *Pilgrim's Progress* and how he journeyed toward the kingdom of God. I felt I just needed to do the same. I had no idea what I was doing – no direction, just a dim chance and a bright hope.

I didn't have any money when I left, so by the third day I was hungry and without shelter. I had made it to

Florida, but it was hot, and I started to become faint. I was standing along the road hitchhiking when I thought I would pass out from the heat, so I took my dog and jumped into the Indian River. The water was warm and brackish. It was not very refreshing, but it cooled my body temperature down. I was worried about Nature, for she had not eaten either. I prayed that the Lord would have favor on us both. Soon after, a man picked me up. He was surprised to find that I had hitchhiked with my dog to Florida. He asked me if I was hungry, and then he bought Nature and I a sandwich. I was so thankful for this, and knew God had answered my prayer.

I ended up in Vero Beach, Florida. I knew about a coffee house that was in town, so I went there for an evening service. I stood in the back at first, unnoticed. Then a girl came up to me after the service and handed me an envelope, telling me that the Lord had spoken to her heart and she wanted to give me something. Inside was some money, and I was able to celebrate by eating a good meal with Nature.

Some other Christians asked me if I had a place to stay, and they invited me to their home when they found that I had just arrived. The house was a place for young people who wanted to be involved in ministry. I didn't know much about them, but my first few weeks there seemed to be what I was looking for. We would witness on the beach to other young people and share our faith with them.

I was able to get some construction work and to be involved with the young people in this ministry. However, I noticed each night as we prayed together that there was much criticism of other Christians. I felt as though one leader was unfairly judging God's people. I knew the church had problems, I had experienced that at home; but to write them all off as this man was doing didn't sit well with me. I started to question things. I knew that most of the Christians in this house were like me, they just wanted to serve God, but this young man seemed to have them under his thumb. I was beginning to think about leaving when some of the men cornered me and told me that I was being rebellious and was going to meet God's wrath if I left. I knew right then and there that I was involved with something that was not of God, and I had to flee.

Early one morning I wrote a note explaining my decision, and that I thought they were under the hands of a tyrant, a false prophet, and they needed to repent and return to their first love. I headed to the freeway going north. I was on the main freeway when a car pulled over. I thought it was a ride, but it was one of the members of that house. He told me that if I did not return I would be killed before I reached the North; that I was disobedient to the Lord and was out of His favor. I told him that the god he talked about was not the God I knew, and that I would never return to such bondage. He left disappointed, and I headed north, relieved.

The time spent in this place was a learning experience for me, for I soon realized how men do control men, that false prophets such as the one in this house where I stayed were as numerous as locusts in a field of crops. The experience in Vero Beach planted keenness in my heart and watchfulness in my soul. I know now that it was all God's grace, and that the devil will do all he can to bring God's people back into bondage. Legalism is such an ugly thing. It is a monster that never satisfies, and it keeps its victims in constant despair. Those trapped by its chains are always trying to pay a debt they cannot pay.

I was learning through all of my experiences, and felt as though I were living *Pilgrim's Progress*. The lessons Christian learned in the book I was experiencing in one-way or another in my life. There have been hard lessons along the way and many difficulties I have brought upon myself. The snares and traps that this world and the devil throw at us often slow us down and even trap us for a season. Nonetheless, God's faithfulness is unfaltering, His mercy is everlasting, and they are new every morning.

Chapter 23

I traveled north. This time I did not go to Michigan. Instead, I headed to Pennsylvania, where I knew a friend of mine lived – a young man that I had met in Michigan who I had led to the Lord. It was now late September, early October, and it was difficult hitchhiking north, as the weather was changing. One night I had to sleep in the cold and rain. I awoke with a terrible cough that did not leave me for weeks. As I think back, I realize that I must have had pneumonia. I made it to Greensburg, Pennsylvania, tired and hungry.

I called Greg, and his family came and picked me up. They took me to their home. It was beautiful. I had never stayed in such a nice place. Greg's parents, Herb and Nancy, were Christians, and they treated me like family. They told me I could stay with them as long as I wanted to.

Soon after arriving in Greensburg, I applied for a job as a photographer in the plant where Herb served as vice president. I was hired, given my own office, my own secretary, and a position I thought I could have never acquired. Months passed and I did my job; I liked the work, yet inside I was restless.

We started a fellowship in Greg's parents' Christian bookstore. This was what I enjoyed the most. At work things started to change. I was flying in small leer jets doing photography at other factories that were affiliated with ours. I was even told that I might be going to Russia. But I didn't seem to fit in. Most of the people I worked with seemed to stay away from me. I know that being a Christian did not go along with their lifestyles.

I was also assigned to trade shows, and would go to Chicago, Houston, and other big cities where I had to help set up. Another part of my job was to rent large rooms in the finest hotels where the shows were being held, hire a bar tender, and purchase all of the alcohol for the parties at night. After the trade shows, the executives met together and discussed each other's products. I did not enjoy this. I felt I was compromising. I was told that even if the men requested women for 'entertainment,' that it was my responsibility to locate them. I wanted nothing to do with this. I approached my boss, who was the head of my department, and told him that I no longer wanted to do the trade shows. He said that it was in my contract, and that if I didn't perform that part of my job, I would be fired. He gave me the choice to do the job or leave, so I left. I did not ask Herb to intervene, because I hired on my own and I knew that it would not be right to get him involved. He was a good Christian man who stood up for his principles, and I looked up to him. I knew that this had to be my choice, and I knew that there were those who questioned my decision. I had never in my life had such a good job, or such an opportunity for advancement, and it seemed as if I were throwing it all away. The Gerhard family had been wonderful to me, and I will always be grateful for their love and support.

Chapter 24

I decided to go back to Michigan. I took what money I had saved and headed northwest toward "home," yet when I arrived, I had no place to call home, no job, and very little money. Jim invited me to stay with him again, and we started attending my old fellowship. I soon moved into the Shalom house, and lived down in the cellar with some other friends.

I sold my car and bought a motorcycle. I liked riding bikes; liked the wind in my face as I drove down long country roads – it was something I had done since I was fifteen. I started riding with other Christians, and we began to witness to outlaw motorcycle clubs. We even started our own club, but I soon tired of this and didn't feel very sure about what we were doing.

One day I went to a restaurant with some friends. A very sweet, young waitress waited on us, and something about her seemed different. I remember when we prayed over our food she looked at us oddly. I think she thought we were mocking God. Since we had driven up on our bikes, we looked like a bunch of outlaw bikers, and not like "normal" Christians. One of the guys recognized her from a church he had attended. I learned that she was a Christian.

Daily, I went to that restaurant for breakfast. It was not the food that I so excitedly looked forward to. I really liked this girl, and soon learned that her name was Julie. Everything about her was attractive to me, yet I felt reserved. I carried around such a degrading image of myself, always reminded of my past failures, and I thought, "Who would want someone like me?" I knew that Jesus Christ had accepted me, but I also knew that the world shunned people with a past like mine; even those who confessed to be Christians would, too.

One day I worked up enough courage up to invite her to a fellowship at a friend's house. She agreed. I was excited. Our first night at that gathering we were both quiet. She was as reserved as I was, but I knew this girl was a precious jewel and that my heart was quickly falling in love.

We started to date often, calling each other and attending church services. I tried to break it off once, because I knew her family disapproved. A pastor told them that I had ruined my life, and that I need not ruin hers. I was crushed within, and wondered if the church would ever accept me.

Months went by and we continued to see each other. We knew there were going to be difficulties with a past such as mine, but we both felt that the Lord had brought us together. Julie's life was so different from mine. She had grown up loving God, was a good student and a good daughter. She had never even drunk a cup of coffee. We were like day and night. I knew I was a new creation in Christ, but I wondered if my past would always haunt me.

Chapter 25

Two years passed before her father agreed on our marriage. I knew her parents were not sure, but we were. I married Julie in the cold month of November 1980, but my heart could not have been any warmer than it was on that day. She was a beautiful, radiant bride; her humility, softness, and gentleness seemed to illuminate from her at every movement. This was a great day for me to be wed to such a precious jewel as Julie. I look back as I write this and not one day do I regret. She is my best friend, my love, and my wife.

Our first year was difficult. We tried living in Northern Michigan, but the photography job I worked for was seasonal. We moved back down state where I worked different jobs. I did not have much to offer my young bride, but she seemed to always beam with joy, never complaining.

We spent our first anniversary in Northern Michigan. The time was spent just enjoying each other. It was cold outside, but our hearts were filled with warmth. Our lives were simple and we had very little, but we had each other. Soon after our anniversary, we learned that Julie was pregnant. We were so excited. I told her we would have a boy, and I felt that the Lord gave me the name of Micah, after the prophet of the Old Testament. I was so sure that it was going to be a boy, that I would not let her pick a girl's name.

Micah was born in the month of August 1982. I had my boy, and I couldn't have been any prouder. We were living in an apartment at the time. I was working in photography, and Julie worked hard making a nice home for our family. She used whatever we had and made it feel as though we lived in a palace. I knew I did not deserve such a precious gift.

Shortly after we were married, Julie's father died a tragic death, and this devastated her. She was so close to her father, and the loss was almost unbearable for her. If the Lord had not carried her through, I do not know what would have happened. Little Micah filled that void. My wife loved every second with this bundle of life. I had never known a mother's love such as hers, and each day I found myself so moved by her endless love and patience.

I continued to go from job to job, nothing seemed to interest me, and I felt as though a driving force within would just not let me settle. I wanted so much to be in missions work, but I felt that was beyond my reach. It was only the elite. I continued street witnessing and was involved in church activities, but it was not enough.

I was receiving newsletters and tracts from Last Days Ministry. I had been very much influenced by their founder, a young musician and minister, Keith Green. He was a voice of challenge for many Christians. Soon after Micah was born, I heard on the Christian radio that Keith and two of his children, along with a missionary family of five were killed in a plane accident near their ministry in Lindale, Texas. This saddened my heart because his zeal and fire for the Lord was so contagious.

Months later I read in one of the newsletters about a mission school in Reynosa, Mexico. This was a school that Keith had helped start. I prayed about going and talked with Julie. We decided we would try to go, so I sent away for an application and we started saving our money. We were accepted and prepared ourselves to leave, but didn't receive any encouragement from the fellowship one way or another. We were on our own, and we knew that many would not understand our decision. Micah was only about a year old, and we soon learned that Julie was pregnant again, but we didn't tell anyone. We knew that this would only make it more difficult.

The day came to leave. I had an old Jeep Wagoner, and we loaded what we needed in it, and started heading for Texas. We even brought Nature with us; we weren't sure how they would receive us if we brought our dog, but we didn't know anyone that we could leave her with. The day we arrived it was near evening. We had traveled to Hidalgo, Texas, which was located right on the border of Mexico. The ministry had a compound in Hidalgo, and this is where we reported. Here we were assigned to move into a small trailer with another family who were staff members at the mission. I soon learned that because I was married, I had to stay in the trailer and walk to Mexico daily for school and training. The single students lived in Mexico.

Getting into a routine was difficult the first few days. I usually left by six in the morning and arrived home about six in the evening. The walk was about three or four miles.

The classes were also difficult for me at first, as I have never been good at sitting still in a classroom.

Each day we learned about missions, and the lives of many missionaries. We were required to read many books, and to view teachings on video. After the first four hours of class, we went out into the streets of Reynosa, Mexico, and witnessed while practicing our Spanish, something I could never get the hang of. I sometimes teamed up with a girl who was fluent in Spanish, so I could witness and she would translate. This helped me bypass the Spanish. I thought to myself that I would never need it, since I wanted to one-day return to South East Asia, and I knew Spanish would not help me there. I later realized that I should have made more of an effort to learn the Spanish, and that God had opened the door for me to learn at the school for a reason.

Life was hard for Julie; she spent most of her time in a small bedroom with Micah, playing with him and teaching him. The people we lived with were legalistic and often times made it difficult for us; they meant well, but it was not easy for my wife. Julie abided her time alone with her son, and was always glad to see me when I returned from school. Whenever we had outreaches, she would get involved; she also cut hair to help out some of the other students. I knew her pregnancy was uncomfortable, and the heat at times was unbearable, but she never complained.

At one point, all of the students had to travel down to a small city just north of Mexico City. We stayed there for about two weeks. Julie and I stayed with a young Mexican family that was involved with the ministry. We enjoyed our stay there. We got along with them very well, there wasn't any pressure on Julie, and we were able to enjoy the outreach work in this town.

When we returned to Texas, time was getting short, school would soon be over, and then we could head back home. There was really nothing much to go back to, so when school let out we headed for Florida, where my mother was living. I had not seen her since the time I accepted the Lord in her home in Humble, Texas. It was good to be finished with school. I learned a lot, but was now ready to move on. We arrived in Florida where we stayed for a couple of weeks at my mother's, then drove back to Michigan. Julie was close to her time of delivery.

We moved into a house that was attached to the church that we had attended before going to Mexico. There were some others living there too, so we set up a little area in one of the small rooms. We had to locate some mattresses and made a bed on the floor. Soon thereafter, Julie gave birth to a little girl we named Melody Joy. We made a small crib for her, however the cold and drafty house was hard on our newborn and we had to rush her to the hospital. Circumstances were difficult for us during this time, and still Julie never complained.

We soon found an apartment, and I began working at a construction job during the day, and in a furnace store at night. Our newborn, Melody, was a bundle of joy; she always seemed so content, and I enjoyed coming home each day to spend time with her and Micah. Months passed and we tried to do our best with what we had, but the nagging hunger and thirst for missions continued to tug at my spirit. I was restless again.

One day I returned from my day job, and Julie told me that my dog Nature had not returned home. That evening I found her lying dead outside of the furnace store where I worked. My heart was broken; she had been with me for over thirteen years. I buried her in the woods, and I knew I would miss her dearly.

We moved back to the house that the church owned. It seemed like an endless cycle for us. I could not seem to ground myself in the system. Everything I tried seemed to fall apart. Each morning I got on my knees to pray, and I asked for the Lord to show me His will; each night I lay awake wondering what it was I was doing wrong.

One night I awoke with a burning passion to go to Nicaragua. I could not shake it. Each morning as I prayed, the thoughts flooded my mind. I kept hearing a still small voice that seemed to ask: "Will you go?" I knew there was a war going on, that the communists had taken over the country, and that there was much suffering there for the Christians. I had no idea what I would do, or how I would get there. I had no support, and knew but a few who would encourage and pray for me. Nonetheless, I woke my wife one late evening, filled with excitement. I told her, "I'm going to Nicaragua. The Lord wants me to go." She just gently smiled at me, and went back to sleep.

For weeks on end I filled my mind and thoughts with going. Each day the burden grew stronger. I started preparing myself, saving what little money I could. A few friends prayed and encouraged me, yet there were those who criticized and spoke ill of me. I did not expect anybody to understand; I didn't understand myself. All I knew was that God was calling me to go, to trust Him no matter what.

A friend bought me a pair of hiking boots, which meant a lot to me. I felt like they were a part of God's armor, that He was shoeing my feet with the gospel of peace. I tried to figure out a plan – what I would do in Nicaragua, and how I would get there – but nothing came together for me. The day drew near for my departure. Micah was a year and half old, and Melody just six months. I knew it would be a bigger test for Julie than it would be for me. I was leaving her with our small car and some money. It wasn't much, but I knew I had to go.

Chapter 26

I left on the morning of February 5th, 1985. I had some friends who were heading to a mission school in Florida, so I was able to ride with them. The cold, damp rain reflected what I was feeling in my heart. Julie had constantly encouraged me, and stood by me even through the opposition and gossip, but that morning she looked me in the eyes as the tears rolled down her face and she said: "Please don't go." I never felt such pain, such a test as this. I looked at her and told her that I had to, and then I kissed her good-bye. I walked out the door without looking back for fear that I would change my mind.

My ride down to Florida was more depressing than the weather. I questioned my motives, and wondered if I was really hearing the voice of the Lord, or just my own misguided wishes. When I arrived in Florida it was bright and sunny. My first stop was at my mother's, where I called Julie. She was cheerful, but I could tell that she wanted me to come home. While at my mother's, I visited a Missionary Alliance church in New Smyrna Beach, Sal. the young pastor there, was a great encouragement. I asked him if he would visit my mother when I left Florida. He said that he would, and my mother and brother, Dennis, came to know the Lord because of his visits. I look back now and realize that for this reason alone, it was worth leaving my home and family in Michigan.

While in Florida I worked on a fishing boat with Tim Myers. He knew much about the conflict in Nicaragua, and told me about the Mosquito Indians that had been persecuted by the communists. He told me that their villages were burned and pastors had been killed. The Indians had fled across the river into the jungles of Honduras, had formed a small army, and were now fighting the communists. I asked him how I could get there; he showed me a map of Honduras and pointed his finger to an obscure part of the world that I had never heard of. The Indians were in the jungles along the Mosquito Coast of Honduras (hence, the name "Mosquito" Indians). I soon found that there were no roads back to this area; I had to find a way in either by air or by sea.

I asked Tim if he knew any contacts. He gave me the name of a missionary who lived in La Cieba, Honduras. This man was supposed to know about the Indians that were being persecuted. Tim gave me the man's phone number, and told me that he didn't know if the man was still living in Honduras anymore. This was all I had to go on, just a phone number and a place on a map. However, I felt this was where the Lord was leading me.

I worked on the boat with Tim for a few days, made some money, then started to hitchhike out of Florida. It was a long trip. At first I was excited and filled with anticipation. I witnessed to everyone who picked me up. One young Christian who gave me a ride invited me to his home; I had dinner with his family and they asked me to spend the night. The next day I was back on the freeway heading west. I was in the Panhandle of Florida when things became grim. The weather changed, and much of the time I was cold and wet.

I stood for hours without a ride. Finally, I was picked up and had a long ride to Louisiana. It was near midnight when I was dropped off in the middle of the freeway, just outside of a rest stop. It was still cold and rainy, and I stood there in the rain, sulking. I questioned myself, thinking that this was all crazy, and wondered who I was kidding. How could God use such a fool like me? Who hitchhikes to the mission field, anyway? Hitchhiking was something I did when I was a hippie; Christians don't do this, I thought to myself. I wasn't feeling very encouraged. I began to think of my home, my children, and Julie, who I missed dearly. I thought of the morning I left and how she had asked me not to go. I felt I should have listened. The rain was coming down harder, and there was no one in sight. I walked to the rest stop and found a phone. I was going to call Julie and tell her that I was coming home, that I had made a stupid mistake.

The phone rang a couple of times before her soft voice answered, "Hello?" "Julie," I said, "it's me, and I want to come home." I was waiting for her to reply that she was excited and expected her to say something like, 'It's about time you woke up.' Instead there was a short silence, then she spoke softly yet confidently, and said: "No, the Lord wants you to go on."

This was not what I wanted to hear. I thought that I had had enough and had learned my lesson, but she was so forward in her convictions, and I saw a side of Julie I had never known. She encouraged me that night, told me how much she loved me, and that the children were doing fine. I did not know the trials that she was going through at the time – the gossip and laughter that was aimed at her behind closed doors, purposely loud enough for her to hear. She never said one negative thing; instead she encouraged me to press on and to see it through.

That night I crawled under a cement picnic table and covered myself with my sleeping bag. I rested there in the rain, thinking about all that had happened. When I awoke the next morning, the sun was out, the air was warm, the birds were singing, and I felt refreshed. I had a renewed zeal within, and I thought of all that had been said during my phone conversation with Julie. I knew that God was in control, no matter how dark things had seemed.

Chapter 27

I made it to Texas, where I stayed with my cousin Joe in San Antonio. He and his wife, Karen, were a great blessing. They took me in and found a job for me for a week, and encouraged and prayed with me. Their Christian testimony was a breath of fresh air. Joe always seemed to be abounding with joy. His home was like an oasis. His wife and family shared all they had with me. I was finding along the way that there were those who truly lived the Christian faith and didn't just talk about it.

It seemed my time with Joe and Karen was too short; however, I knew I needed to go. I couldn't get too comfortable. There was a task ahead, even though I did not know what it was, or what means were at my disposal to accomplish it, and the driving hunger to press on was relentless. I knew that I was to count all things as loss, that it was one thing to say I trusted Jesus, and another to put it to the test. I was learning that no matter what was before me, that it was His business, not mine. Like Peter, I was to step out of the boat with confidence, and to step out in the midst of storms in faith. Even though I had failed by allowing the storms to frighten me, His hand had been there to reach out and pull me through. Though I am faithless at times, Jesus is always faithful.

I took a Greyhound bus down to Hidalgo, Texas, where Julie and I had previously attended the mission school. I stayed there for a few days before entering Mexico, then continued my journey on to Honduras.

I took a bus to Mexico City. From there I was not sure which way to go. I knew about a missionary in the Jungles of Belize, so decided to head there first. The trip became difficult from this point on. The bus trips were in old school busses packed to twice their capacity. People carried live chickens, fruits, vegetables, and whatever else they could carry. The smell was unbearable, and the heat was starting to take its toll on me.

I arrived at the Belize border early in the evening. By then I was regretting that I had not studied Spanish harder when I was in the mission school. I was thankful that the Mexican people were kind and patient with me along the way, because I had no idea where I was and how to get where I was going.

I walked across the border and received my visa at the customs station, then climbed back on another crowded bus heading toward Belize City, the capitol of this tiny country. I was happy to find that in Belize many of the people spoke English. The British had ruled this country for many years, and it was formally called "British Honduras."

In Belize I found a little hotel room with a shower in the hall. I sat on the bed and thought about all that I had gone through and how far I had come. I started to think that maybe God was testing me, and that I could go home now. I missed my family very much. I took my camera bag out and was going to clean my camera when I found, inside of my bag, a handkerchief wrapped around something. I opened it up, and inside were some caramels. Julie knew I liked caramels. On the handkerchief she had drawn a heart, and in the center of the heart she had written: "We love you very much – Julie, Micah, and Melody." My eyes filled with tears, my stomach was all in knots. God had blessed me with such a wonderful family, and I was so far away from them.

That night I listened to a tape I had in my small cassette player, and heard a song about a bondservant. I knew that in the Bible, Paul the apostle called himself a bondservant of Christ. I also knew that in the Old Testament, a bondservant did twice the work of a hired hand, because he did it out of love. That night as I prayed, I told the Lord I wanted to be a bondservant, and that if I never saw my family again, that I was willing to go on and trust Him. I cried that night, my heart broken, as all of my selfish ambitions were laid before Him. I wanted to be free from all that would hinder me from giving myself to the One who loved me and gave His life for me. I knew that night that I was to press on no matter what the cost, or what others thought.

Chapter 28

The next day I boarded another one of those infamous buses. This time we headed down the jungle roads of Belize. The bus driver knew about the missionary, and told me that he would inform me when to get off. We traveled most of the day with one flat tire before we reached the mission compound. The driver yelled that it was time for me to get off. I grabbed my backpack and camera and got off. The bus left me in a cloud of dust, and I stood in the middle of the dirt road wondering what to do next.

Off in the distance I saw a trail leading to a large house made from the trees of the forest. It had a large thatched roof, and other small huts stood nearby. I knew this was the place.

I saw a young man conversing with one of the local natives; I approached and waited for him to finish his conversation. He barely took notice of me, as though I were not even there. As I stood waiting, I looked down at the ground, and right at the toe of my hiking boots was a tarantula being eaten by a swarm of red ants. It was not a very appealing sight, and certainly not a warm introduction to this jungle compound.

Finally the man came over and introduced himself to me. I told him what I was trying to do, as much as I could explain, anyway. He welcomed me in. The director of the compound was out of the country. This young man was with his family – a wife and two boys. They had been working with the local Indians for a few years.

They stood out from among the Indians with their light blonde hair.

That night we sat down to a dinner of boiled armadillo. I can't say that it was the most appetizing meal that I have ever had, but it was filling. In the evening the man took me to a remote village, to a small hut that served as the chapel. There was one oil lamp hanging from a rope from the bamboo rafters. The smell of the oil was strong. The village people came out for the service, and this young man preached in their tongue. I could see that he had a burden for these people. He told me later that this village had been growing marijuana for resale. It was the only way they had to make a living. He had a hard task ahead of him, trying to show them the way of Christ, and to another means of income.

That night the young missionary told me that I could sleep in one of the small huts, but warned me about scorpions in the thatch above my cot. He said: "Sometimes they fall on you in the night."

I have learned over the years now that missionaries can have a sense of humor that can be trying at times. That night I lit a candle by my bunk and stayed awake watching the thatch roof as bats flew in and out of my open window. I really felt I was at the end of my trip, that somehow this was all a test, and that maybe I had passed. I was running out of money and still did not know where I was going or how to get there. I prayed that night for a sign.

The next morning I asked the missionary to take me to the port village where I could use a phone to call out of the country. I prayed that morning that if I called the number in Honduras that was given to me by Tim Myers in Florida, and I reached the man who knew about the Mosquito Indians, I would go on. If not, I was going home. I dialed the number, thinking the guy would not even be around. It rang only once, and a man's voice answered. I said, "Hello, my name is Tom." Before I could say anything else, he said: "I've been expecting you."

I was shocked, to say in the least. He didn't even know me. I could not believe my ears. I soon found out that Tim had gotten a hold of him and told him that I was on my way. I knew when I hung up that I was going to make it to the Mosquito Coast. I called Julie; it was good to hear her voice. I told her what had happened, and she shared my excitement, though she never mentioned the difficulties she was having at home.

The next morning I took a ferry to a Guatemala port and from there I traveled by bus to Honduras. I finally reached La Cieba, Honduras, after a few days of travel. I met the man Tim had told me about, the man I had talked to on the phone in Belize. He picked me up where the bus had dropped me off, and we went to his home. I remember emptying out my backpack so I could wash my clothes, and found I had a hitchhiker with me – a scorpion jumped out of my pack. By now I was getting used to the environment; it was much like Vietnam.

That night my new acquaintance told me all that he knew about the Mosquito Indians. I soon learned, however, that he had never been back to the jungles where the Indians had their camps. I did not feel very comfortable with this man. Instead of encouraging me, he tried to discourage me. He said there was only one flight out to the jungles per week, and that they were booked for months in advance. He also told me that the plane landed in a village called Puerto Lempira, a village controlled by the Honduran military. He said they were watchful of any strangers because of the conflict in Nicaragua. He also told me that the Indians were held up in the jungles a long way from Puerto Lempira, and not having any contacts, it would be nearly impossible for me to be taken back in. I listened patiently, but I knew God had not brought me this far only to turn back. I asked his friend to type me a letter of introduction in Spanish for the Indians in case I did run across them.

The next day we went to the airstrip. The man at the counter told me that there was no room on the flight, but I was not about to give up, even though the missionary told me that I was wasting my time. I waited around, and watched them load the plane. It was an old Second World War DC-3 prop plane that held about thirty-five people. It looked like I was not going to make it, but just as I was about to leave; the man told me they had one more space. I boarded the plane, and it rumbled off down the strip and into the blue skies over Honduras.

The plane was crude, and grumbled all the way. There were no seat belts, and the heat was causing the sweat to roll down my face. It took about two hours to reach Puerto Lempira. The plane made a bumpy landing on a dirt airstrip.

I could see a village off in the distance on the shore of a large lagoon. I jumped off the plane and waited for a man to throw my backpack to me. Soon thereafter the plane departed, and I found myself watching as the other passengers headed toward the village. I had no idea what to do next or where to go. I didn't even know what the Indians looked like, and the words of that man rang in my ears: "Don't trust anyone."

I headed toward the village not thinking too clearly; I remember walking past a checkpoint where two soldiers with machine guns were standing behind some sand bags. All I could think of saying was, "Ola," meaning "hello" in Spanish. They watched me walk right by them. Being a former soldier, I should have known that this was a checkpoint, and that I was supposed to stop, but I didn't. They just looked at me as though I were some crazy "gringo." I must have been a strange sight: unshaven face, grubby Levi's, and a backpack. I was surely not someone from their part of the world.

As I walked through the village, wondering what to do next, I noticed an older man walking toward me. His expression was hardened, as though he had been through much in his life. I thought to myself, "He looks like an Indian." I stopped him, and handed him the letter. He read it without one change of expression, then took my letter and walked away without saying a word. I stood there confused, not knowing what else to do. I decided to walk in the same direction that he had gone in.

About twenty minutes later he returned with another man, a man much younger then he. This man spoke some

English. He told me that he was an Indian; he said he was a Contra, a "freedom fighter."

They took me to a cement block building and interrogated me. They wanted to know who I was, and why I wanted to visit the Indians. I really did not have much to say. I told them I was a Christian and that I was concerned about the plight of the Indians. I was informed that I would meet one of their leaders and that it would be up to him whether I were allowed to go back into the jungles with them.

That night I slept in the cement block building, on the floor along with everything that crawled around in the night. The mosquitoes were horrendous, and the black flies seemed to have chosen me for their nightly meal. I was given some beans and rice, which I gratefully consumed, for I had not eaten since I had left La Cieba.

Chapter 29

I met the commander the next day. He was a kind but stern man, who told me about the trials and struggles of his people. I was told that all of their villages had been burned and that many of the Indians were in Communist concentration camps. He also told me that the Honduran military treated them roughly and would take anything away from them that they wanted for themselves. I felt that the Indians were a peaceful people until the war brought devastation to all they had known.

I was allowed to travel back to the jungles with them. Early the next morning we loaded into a small Toyota pickup truck. Three of us crammed in the front, and about six Indians in the back, riding in the bed of the truck. They also loaded some beans and rice that they had purchased into the bed of the truck. It was hard to believe that this little truck could handle such a load. The road we traveled on was no more than a two-track.

The going was rough, with a lot of bumps along the way. We traveled through thick jungles that hung over the trails like a great canopy. Beautiful birds sat in the trees like ornaments, and flocks of parrots flew from treetop to treetop, squawking as if they were complaining to one another. It was a beautiful but difficult environment.

It wasn't long before we came upon a military checkpoint. The Honduran soldiers asked the Indians for their papers, and then they asked for my passport. I knew they were curious about me, and wondered why I was going back with the Indians. I suspected they thought

I was with the CIA, or some military advisement from the US government. They seemed to be satisfied with my credentials and sent us on our way after confiscating an army issue canteen that they found behind the driver's seat. I discovered that if the Indians carried anything that looked like military issue, it was to be seized from them. The Honduran government did not want to acknowledge that they had Contras in their country who were not only hiding out, but who were also operating training camps in their jungles. This, however, was what was happening.

After about six hours of traveling through the rough terrain and a few more checkpoints, we came to a river called Rus-Rus. There we drove onto an old barge; it was tied to a heavy rope that was anchored to large trees on both sides of the embankment. We pulled ourselves across, and then drove the truck onto the dry embankment.

When we drove off the barge, it felt as though we entered another world. Things changed; the Indians who came to meet us each carried a rifle and had grenades strapped to their ammo belts, along with extra rifle rounds. They were dressed in worn-out clothing, and most didn't have any shoes on their feet. They were threatening in appearance. Their faces seemed to be without emotion, as if they were made numb by the horrors of war. I found out later, however, that most of them were kind and thoughtful.

I knew this sight; this feeling was all so familiar. I remember thinking to myself: "I can't believe it – I'm back." I felt as though I had just traveled back in time, and was standing in the jungles of Vietnam. The heat, sweat, and the smell of gun grease filled my senses with memories that I had tried to forget. I knew that God had brought me to this place. I thought back to the beginning and all I had gone through to get here, and it was truly God's hand that made the way clear. However, here I stood: very little money, no relief supply, no Christian material, and I could speak very little Spanish. I thought: "Here I am Lord…now what?"

The young Indians escorted me down a jungle path to a small compound made up of a number of bamboo huts that were about five feet off the ground, built upon stilts made from the forest. I even noticed young girls, who were no more than sixteen years old, carrying rifles. They all had their eyes glued upon me, wondering who I was and what I was doing in such a place as this. They took me into a hut and showed me a hammock; I understood that this was my bed. I took off my pack, loaded my camera, and started to take some pictures of my surroundings.

Soon after, I met a young man dressed in camouflage fatigues. He spoke English well. I found out that he was the doctor for the Indians. He took me to their medical hut and showed me their supply; it was very little, and most had been damaged from being transported so far back into the jungles. I asked him about the Indians. He shared with me that his father had been a pastor, but had died the year before. He told me that many years back, Moravian missionaries had established churches among the Indians. I had learned of the Moravians and their zeal for the Lord from mission school.

I came to understand that these Indians had a strong Christian upbringing, which caused the communists to hate them even more; the fact that they were native Indians was also a strike against them. (Prejudice is an ugly snake whose venom spares no one.)

My first evening with the Indians, I sat in my hammock, barefooted like my host. I started conversing with whoever could understand me. One soldier was squatting down in front of me as we tried to make conversation. I started to put my feet down on the floor, when he nonchalantly reached his hand forward as if to say: "stop." I froze for a moment and watched him pull out a big knife as he moved in my direction. I heard a whack, and then he motioned for me to continue. Right under my bare feet, where I almost stood, was a large black scorpion. I was thankful for this young man, but later found that scorpions seemed to be attracted to me, and I did not always get by without getting stung. The jungles crawled with all kinds of dangerous snakes, spiders, and other creatures who liked to roam in the night. One night I even came upon a jaguar.

The night was pitch black. I lay in the hammock thinking of family and friends. My candle soon burned out, and I laid awake thinking about all that had happened. I do not know when I dozed off, but I do remember waking to the sound of singing. It was still pitch black out, but I could hear voices as if they were praying. I grabbed my flashlight, glanced at the floor before I jumped out of my hammock, slipped on my hiking shoes, and went outside.

Mosquito Coast Indians (Contras)

I scanned the surrounding compound with my flashlight, and soon came across a group of Indians upon their knees. Some were holding their rifles, but each head was bowed, and there was great intensity upon each face as they cried out their prayers. I was truly moved. I realized that these people had a love for God. I did not know how many of them truly understood the meaning of God's grace and mercy, or what it meant to be born again. However, I could tell that whoever the missionaries were that had visited these people many years before, they had obviously planted a good seed of truth. This sight took me in; I could not help but weep along with them. I got on my knees and began to pray for them. I felt so inadequate, coming all this way with nothing to share with them. I asked the Lord to give me a sign, to show me why I was there. I didn't even have any idea how I was getting home, or if I ever would. I just knew that I had to be there for a reason.

Chapter 30

The next day I learned more from the doctor about the Indians. Being Moravians, they did not believe in taking up arms. They were taught to be pacifist. However, when the communists started destroying their villages and killing their people, many took up arms and started the resistance. This was a dilemma for them because of their beliefs. It also burdened my heart with a greater compassion for these people.

That day they took me to villages that were hidden in the jungles. I was told that the Sandinistas, the communists, would sometimes cross the river and try to locate these villages and kill some of the people. Most of the people had very little clothing; children's stomachs were swelled from malnutrition and parasites. Their food source was scarce, except for the bananas and coconuts they could find alongside the river embankment in the trees.

They also took me to a training camp, which they did not allow many outsiders to see. They seemed to trust me, as if they were hoping that I could do something, that I could be a voice for them. I started to think that maybe this was my purpose, to let others know of the plight of the Indians.

In the training camp, my heart was pierced through by the things that I encountered. There were young boys, some hardly over ten years old, training for battle. These little refugees had lost their parents, and I could tell by many of their faces that they had bitterness and vengeance in their hearts. I did not like this sight. I knew that God did not want men killing each other, let alone children armed with machine guns and hand grenades. I took some photos of their faces. Even today, these prints are a haunting reminder of the horrors of war and how men can stoop to such low forms of degradation and hatred.

Indians in prayer

I thought of Vietnam, of those young faces and the horrors they had encountered. God had brought me back into the battlefield, and I knew this time it was for the souls of men. I tried as often as I could to witness through an interpreter, to share the love of God with these people. Many wanted to pray and most wanted the war to end; they just wanted to go home and live in peace.

Mosquito Coast - Young Soldier

One night the soldiers set up a small generator and strung a piece of electrical wire in a tree. Then they hooked up a crude light bulb. The light was dim, but it instantly attracted every flying insect for miles around. I felt as though I had no more blood to give, and surrendered to the never-ending onslaught of mosquitoes and black flies. The soldiers brought in a little table and placed it under the light. I knew there was going to be a meeting of some sort. Soon men and women alike came and sat on the ground. I wondered what was next. I thought they were possibly going to have a military strategy meeting or something of that order. I was surprised to see how wrong I was.

An older, raggedly dressed gentleman, holding a Bible that was even more ragged than his clothes, stood under the dim light. He opened with a word of prayer, then carefully and gently opened his Bible. He treated it as though he had gold in his hands, and in a sense, he did! I had never seen a Bible so ragged and worn as this. It was missing the cover, and he protected it as though it were even more important than his own life. How I wished at that moment that I had some Spanish Bibles. I was disappointed that I had nothing to give him.

He spoke with a gentle voice as he shared from the Word of God to his people. I sensed no animosity or hatred. I could not understand what he was saying, but I could feel the gentle breeze of the Holy Spirit blow through the compound. I knew that this man was trying to reach these young souls with the Truth. I wondered how it would be if I were in his shoes – would I have the same gentle spirit, or would I be filled with hatred and vengeance for my enemy? I will never forget that night as long as I live.

Chapter 31

The next day I sat on the porch of my hut, thinking about the events of the night before. I still felt so inadequate, and even more, as I saw such need in these people. I wanted so badly to hand that pastor a good Bible, to supply him with all of the study material he needed. The doctor told me that the communists had confiscated the Bibles from the Indians, and had even used the pages for toilet paper. I started to understand why God had brought me to this place.

That same day I noticed a squad of men coming in from the jungles. You could tell that they had been on a long journey. These were men who had been in battle. I could not help but remember my days in the War, and the intensity and fear that came along with the fighting. I scanned the faces of these young men, and wondered how many knew about the loving mercy of Christ?

I noticed one man who was dressed in camouflage fatigues; he stood out from among the rest. He seemed well distinguished, and I knew he was a leader. I was soon introduced to this man, whose name was Wilfrado. He spoke very good English, and was the commanding officer of the troops. Wilfrado was well educated, and had been studying to be a doctor in the university before the communists took over the government and kicked the Indians out of school. He also told me that his father had been a Moravian pastor and had died the year before.

I appreciated my time with this man. He didn't seem to have a mean streak in him. He was kind and considerate, and wanted to know about me and about my beliefs. We talked much about the grace of God, and I knew this young man had a true relationship with the Lord. He talked about his home, his schooling, and his desire to fulfill his education. He never mentioned the communists or the fighting that I knew he had encountered.

One morning I asked Wilfrado what the needs of his people were. They primarily needed medical supplies, food, and clothing. I said to him, "If I can make it back home, what can I bring to you that you need the most?" I waited for his reply, as he silently stood considering my question. I was expecting to hear a list of material goods, but he looked me squarely in the eyes and said: "I would like to have eight hundred pocket-sized Spanish New Testaments, with Psalms and Proverbs for my men, and a full Bible with concordance and dictionary for me and my brother." I remember his face as if it were today. He spoke this request, then looked at me as if to say, "Are you really concerned? Will you do this for us?"

I knew right then and there that God had taken me from my family, all the way through the jungles of Honduras, because there were men who hungered for His Word. This was why I had come, and I knew this was why I had to return.

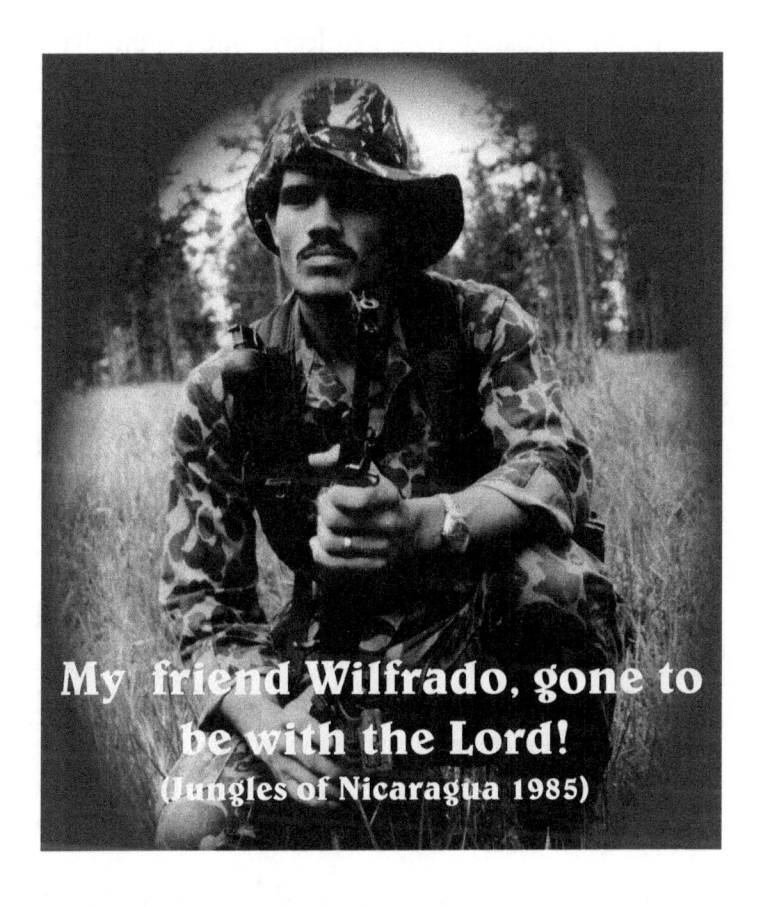

My friend Wilfrado, gone to be with the Lord!
(Jungles of Nicaragua 1985)

Chapter 32

I soon prepared myself to leave, but I didn't have a way to get back. The small Toyota truck had left on the first day it dropped me off. The Indians took me to the barge, and I crossed the river. They told me that sometimes the Peace Corps came to the river to check on things, and that maybe I would run into them and catch a ride back out of the jungles. This was all I had to go on.

When I crossed the river, I found a place to sit under a tree and I waited. Evening came quickly, along with all of the strange sounds of the jungle. I was not too keen on spending the night under a tree, but night was coming on fast, and I prepared myself to sit all night in the jungle alone. Not long thereafter, however, I thought I could hear a vehicle off in the distance. Sure enough, a truck came down the road carrying two men. I approached them, and they agreed to take me to their compound. I was relieved; I didn't want to bunk with the creatures of the night.

At the Peace Corps compound I met a tall Texan. He invited me to get something to eat in their mess hall, and told me that the next day they would take me to Puerto Lempira where I could catch the flight back to La Cieba. That night I was able to sleep on a mattress and also eat something besides beans and rice. I was glad to be returning, but my heart ached for all that I had seen and learned from the Indians. I thought about Wilfrado's request, and his quizzical expression, as he wondered if I would really return.

In La Cieba, I returned to the missionary's house where I had learned about the Indians. I wondered how I would get home, as I had but a few dollars, and the thought of traveling all the way back by land soured my stomach.

The Lord knew of my need even before I did. The missionary's mother was visiting him from Canada, and told me that she would pay for my flight to Miami, Florida. I could reimburse her when I returned home. All she asked was that I send it to her Canadian address.

I was informed that flights into Miami were booked, as it was almost Easter, and many people were traveling. I packed the next morning, anyway, and went to the airport. I asked if my name could be put on standby. The man at the counter told me that mine was the last name on the list; nevertheless, I knew I would make it home. I had not seen my family in months, and somehow I knew that I would be home for Easter. The flight arrived and I waited patiently; at the last moment, when it seemed I would not be going, the man told me there was an opening.

The flight was only two hours to Miami. I couldn't help thinking about how long and how difficult it had been for me to get to Honduras; and now my return was uneventful and relatively short. I was so thankful. I knew I was a sight to look upon. I had given most of my clothing to the Indians, and they, in turn, had given me some camouflage fatigues. I looked as though I had just returned from guerrilla warfare. I also had two machetes that were given to me by the Indians that I had tied to my backpack. I felt like I reflected the environment that I came out of, and I felt good.

Once in Miami, I didn't know what to do next. I thought about hiking to the freeway and trying to catch a ride north. Then I remembered that a friend of mine had moved to Coral Gables, right outside of Miami. Glen was the one I had gone on my first mission trip to Mexico. I found his number in the phone book, and his wife came to pick me up. Glen and his wife opened their home to me, fed me, and we fellowshipped together. Glen seemed very interested in what I had gone through, and told me he would return with me when the time came.

That night I laid awake trying to figure out how to get home, and if I could make it in time for Easter. The next morning Glen surprised me with a car that they had had for sale. They told me that I could have it. Gratefully, I packed the car with my few belongings, and headed north. I only had about twenty-five dollars, but I knew that God had supplied the car, and that he would supply the fuel. I was learning each step along this trip the importance of a surrendered life. I needed to pray each day and to remind myself that God was in control – not me.

On the way north the car started to overheat. I made it to Fort Pierce where Tim lived, the man who first shared with me the plight of the Indians, and who had given me a job on his boat. The car barely made it to his house. I knew something was really wrong. That night I attended a church meeting with Tim. He shared with the people what I had gone through and that I was trying to get home. Over the next few days, some men from the church came and tore apart and then rebuilt the engine. Then one of the church members handed me a one hundred dollar bill, and I was on my way again.

Easter was fast approaching, just hours away. I traveled all day and night, wanting to make it on time. I felt the Lord had surely spoken to my heart and had assured me that I would make it home by Easter morning. I did make it. I pulled into the church – the parking lot was full, and the service was already in progress. There were butterflies in my stomach. I hadn't seen Julie and the children in such a long time. I hadn't even spoken to her in almost a month. I was still dressed in my jungle fatigues when I entered the church. The pastor took a quick glance at me, then proceeded with his message as though I weren't there. I just wanted to see Julie. I didn't care about the looks of disapproval, the smirks, or laughter that seemed to fill the sanctuary. I scanned the pews but did not see her. Finally, a girl came up to me and whispered in my ear, "She's in the nursery."

I quickly left the hall and headed to the nursery. When I walked in, Julie was bending over, comforting a child who seemed to be having a bad day. Here was my wife as I always remembered her – gentle and caring. She turned and saw me, and before I knew it we were embracing. Nothing was said; nothing had to be said. All the tests and trials, all the hurts and lonely nights seemed to vanish in that moment. I do not know how long we held each other, but it felt as though time did not exist – just us. She kissed me, and then I looked around to find young Micah. Happy and carefree, he came and hugged me, as though I had never left. Melody didn't recognize me at first, she was cautious when I first picked her up, but I was so happy to be home and with my family again.

The next few days were a time for refreshing and reacquainting. I enjoyed my time with my family. No one from our church asked about my experience except for a few friends who had known us from the beginning. I didn't expect anyone to understand. How could they? They had not witnessed what I had. I knew also that we were not among the elite of the church – I had learned over the years that pride can make its way even into the church pews. I cared less each day what men thought, and tried to focus my heart on what the Lord wanted. I knew He had called me, and that was all that mattered.

Right away I started on a plan to return. I could not help but see the face of Wilfrado night and day. I thought about the Bibles he asked for, and I started to check into every resource I could find. In the days that followed I threw myself into the preparation with a passion and a zeal that I had never experienced before. There were a few churches that became aware of me, and the local newspaper published an article, including a whole spread of my photo work done in Honduras.* Doors where opening for me, and I was excited that the Lord was making a way for me to return.

(* One note about my interview with the newspaper – I regret speaking out against the communists as I sided with the Indians. I soon found out that some of my statements angered some missionaries who had been working with the Sandinistas, the communists, and realized that some things should never have been said. Jesus died for all men, whether communist, or otherwise. They all need redemption. It was a hard lesson to learn, but one that I am thankful to have learned.)

Chapter 33

I spoke at a few churches and received some support. I started buying supplies. I thought of the Honduran pastor and his ragged Bible, and went out and purchased about twenty leather-bound Spanish study Bibles for the pastors, Wilfrado, and his brother. I wanted to give them the best I could find. I even found some concordances and dictionaries in Spanish. Frank Wash (a friend of mine) and I were able to accumulate over eight hundred Spanish New Testaments with Proverbs and Psalms, as requested.

I kept in contact with Glen, down in Florida, and he worked on getting three tickets from Miami to La Cieba, Honduras. Another man named Joe volunteered to go – he was from one of the churches where I had spoken, and I soon found out that he was a Vietnam Veteran and had been in the same outfit that I was in while stationed in Vietnam. Frank Wash became the fourth one of the team – he was a member from our church, and always upbeat and full of energy. I knew I couldn't have had a better group of men to go with me than these. They didn't need an agenda, or a plan; they were just willing to go.

I approached the pastor of our fellowship and asked him if I could use the hall to put on a meal and concert to raise support. A few friends and my brother, Steve, shared the music that night. Julie, along with the help of her friends, cooked a good meal. We had a good time, and were surprised to have been able to raise about seven hundred dollars that evening.

I remember sitting outside on this warm evening, when one of the church members came and stood before me. I could tell he wanted to tell me something. Finally he spurted out a relentless criticism of me. He told me that he was concerned for my family, and that I was abandoning them. He told me that single people should be doing what I was doing, so I asked him: "Where are the single people, and why are they not going?" Each of the men who had volunteered to go with me was married and had children, with the exception of Frank. I also recalled the missionaries that I had read about, and how they had families and counted all things as loss for Christ. He looked at me again and said: "I am only concerned for your family." I controlled the anger that welled up within me, and I stood to my feet, looked him in the eyes, and asked: "If you are so concerned about my family, how many times did you come and knock on the door when I was gone, and ask my wife if she had any needs?" He just responded that he felt anger from me and turned and walked away.

I was tired of the hypocrisy. I didn't expect anyone to understand, but I knew how hard they had made it for my wife with their gossip and slander. I had to let the Lord deal with my heart that night; I knew I had to get my family away from this place.

Chapter 34

The time came for my return to Honduras. I came home in April, and it was now August. I was so looking forward to going back. This time, however, I would not leave my family behind. I did not want Julie to go through what she had gone through the last time. Glen's wife invited Julie to stay with her in Coral Gables while we were overseas, so we loaded the same car Glen gave us and headed south. Frank and Joe followed in Frank's pick-up. There was an excited anticipation for what lie ahead. I felt such freedom in Christ that I had never known before; happy that God uses the foolish things of the world. I knew I fit into that category, and I was glad.

We made it to Glen's, and made the final preparations for our trip. We packed all of the Bibles in duffel bags, and stuffed the other bags with medical supplies and clothing. We had a large amount of supply for four people to carry, but I knew it was but a 'drop in the bucket' compared to all that the Indians needed. I remember feeling like it was Mission Impossible. I had no idea how we would hook up with the Indians again, and I knew it would be different traveling with four men instead of one. I was afraid the Honduran military could really give us trouble.

The day came to leave. I kissed Julie good-bye, and felt good about leaving her with Glen's wife.

Our flight was comfortable. We made it to La Cieba, and were able to clear customs without a problem, with the exception that when they found out we had Bibles, everyone wanted one. We knew our mission, and only allowed a few to be given out. It's hard to turn anyone away who wants God's Word, no matter the motive.

We found a room in town, and then took a taxi to the airstrip where we needed to catch a flight back into the jungle. As before, we were told that the flight was booked and there were no openings for weeks. I kept thinking about the difficulties ahead for four of us; it's so easy to look at our circumstances and lose heart, instead of looking to the Lord, Who is in control.

The next day we went to the airport and waited, and sure enough we were able to get on board. The flight was hot and bumpy as before. Each of us had sweat rolling down our faces as the plane made its noisy way into the sky. I wondered how to make contact with the Indians again, since the Indians had no idea I was returning. I thought of the military checkpoints and how to get by them. My mind seemed to be consumed with worries, and at that point the mission did seem to be impossible. However, when the plane landed on the dirt airstrip and the door was opened, there waiting on the airstrip was one of the Indian's top officials. He was there to pick up another leader, who did not happen to be on the plane. Our arrival coordinated with his, and he was our ticket in.

That night we slept in a village "hotel." It was constructed out of plank boards. The cots were steel framed, and held ragged mattresses that were draped with yellow, stained sheets. That first night in Puerto Lempira was miserable. The mosquitoes were unbearable.

I remember looking over at Frank, and he had that old yellow sheet draped over his head trying to cut down on the endless onslaught of these tiny vampires. I felt strangely that night, as if it would be a night that I would never forget.

The next day we headed back into the jungles. We reached the barge and crossed, and I soon met up with the doctor. I noticed things had changed some, and that at first they would not allow us back into the camp where I had stayed before. That night we stayed in a small hut by the river. I remember sleeping on top of a bunch of fifty-pound bags of rice and beans. It was not the most comfortable bed I had slept on. We heard some shooting not too far away that night, but were not aware of what was happening.

The next morning the Indians took us to the camp. It was almost deserted. I took a walk with Glen, while Frank and Joe took a nap in their hammocks. Before long, a man with a gun awakened Frank. He was an American. He asked Frank what he was doing there, and told him the camp was surrounded. I guess we had walked into a military coup that was happening among the Indians. It was a crazy situation.

Things soon settled down, and this man, whose name was Sam, told us he was training the Indians. He told us that he had worked in Israel, and in other countries. He denied being a soldier of fortune, but I believe that he was. We told him that we had brought in Bibles and supplies, and he arranged for us to visit the village pastors

Indians and our team - Joe, Frank, Glenn and Myself

where we could share the things we had with them and their people. I asked him if I could come to his training camp to hand out Bibles and tracts to his men, but he told me this was not possible.

I soon tried to locate Wilfrado. I was told he was held up in the jungles of Nicaragua with his men. I located a few men who were going to meet him, and asked them to take the Bibles to Wilfrado and his brother. They agreed, so we loaded them into a dugout tree that they were using as a boat, and they headed off across the Rio Cocoa River into Nicaragua. We spent our days visiting refugee camps and ministering to the pastors and their people. One of my greatest blessings was to find the pastor with the ragged Bible, and give him a new Bible, along with other study material. He was so full of joy to receive these wondrous gifts of God's Word. That one moment, and the knowledge that Wilfrado was to receive his Bibles, was reward enough for everything that I had been through.

One morning a group of soldiers came and took us to the secret training camp where we were able to give out tracts and New Testaments to the young soldiers, many who were not even in their teens. Sam was surprised and upset to see us there, but I knew God's Word was more important then his ego. The day came for us to leave. It was a sad departing. There was so much more to do. We had crossed the river into Nicaragua with these people and had witnessed the burned villages and the churches that had been destroyed, and we knew of all the lives that had been lost. I wanted to return, and somehow knew I would. That last day we found out that Wilfrado had received his Bibles and that he was very pleased that we had returned. I left, feeling that the mission that had at first seemed impossible was accomplished.

Chapter 35

Back in Florida we said good-bye to Glenn and his family. He told me that he wanted to return with me the next time I went. Frank and Joe headed north, while I decided to visit my mother in New Symrna. Julie and I really didn't have a place to return to – we were without a home and without clear direction.

I was pleased to find that my mom was involved in her church, and seemed to be full of the joy of the Lord. Pastor Sal was a good friend to my family, and I saw a wonderful transformation in them.

While at my mom's, I started to think about staying in Florida. Julie was willing, so we prayed about it. Inside, I was growing restless again. The exhilaration from such a wonderful trip soon faded, and I was perplexed as to what to do next. I talked about the mission and how well it went, but something inside was nagging at my heart.

One morning I awoke feeling weak and tired. I didn't know why, I just didn't feel like doing anything. For days I was up and down. One day I felt fine, the next I was drained. I tried to help an older man tar a roof, but didn't last long before I felt sick and had to quit. By evening I felt better, and the next day I took my children to the beach. The sun baked me, and I came down with a fever. By midnight I was shaking and sweating, and couldn't hold anything down. My fever kept rising and I felt I was becoming delirious. The next morning Julie rushed me to the hospital, and on the way there I felt as if my life were slipping away. At the hospital they quickly put me on IV's, and I learned that I had Malaria. I thought of that night in Puerto Lempira, and the strange feeling I had, and I knew that that was the night I was infected with Malaria.

The next few days were up and down; my fever remained high, and someone was sent across state to find the medicine that was needed to treat the Malaria. I laid in bed feeling sick and depressed, and kept thinking about how successful our trip had been. I could not understand why I was suffering.

One night I couldn't sleep. My fever had come down, but I was still feeling faint. I remembered being in my tent in Vietnam, when I heard that voice of warning, and as I lay there, I again heard that still, small voice within. Only this time I heard these words: "This is not an adventure trip, this may cost you your life. Are you willing to pay the price?"

Chapter 36

I was released from the hospital, and started back to Michigan with my family. A few days after returning to Michigan, I had a relapse and ended up in the Veteran's Hospital in Ann Arbor, Michigan. I thought about all that I had gone through and I wondered if I had the heart for more. While lying in the hospital bed, I decided I would find a job and just live the "normal" everyday life, whatever that was.

I found a job in a photography studio. It didn't pay much, but it was something. We still did not have a place of our own and, for the time being, stayed with friends. One day I found an ad in the paper for a house to rent with the option to buy. I didn't have much to work with, but Julie and I prayed, then I called the number listed in the ad.

A man answered: "Hello, this is Bob Lorincz." I soon learned that he was a real estate agent, and that the house happened to be one of his rentals. I told him about our situation, and he agreed to meet with us. I found out that Bob was a Christian. He opened up the house for us and let us move in with very little down. He was very kind to us, and we were grateful for such an opportunity.

Bob became a very close friend. He has, through the years, been a great support in fellowship and prayer. We started to meet together early mornings at his office for prayer and Scripture memorization. I enjoyed this time, and it became a real strength in my Christian walk. However, within my heart I was still struggling with decisions.

I could not forget about the Indians; the desire to return was increasing with each passing day. One day I got on my knees and started to pray. It seemed like everything was falling apart for us – the car was falling apart, the bills were piling up, and it seemed like the harder I tried the worse it became. That morning in prayer, I asked, "Why?" Then that still, small voice that I have come to know as the voice of my Savior spoke gently to my heart: "I have not called you to this."

I knew in that moment that I was to enter fully into the work of the Lord. There was such a release in my heart. I told Julie, and she encouraged me to do as the Lord directed. I immediately started preparing for another trip to Honduras.

At the same time, I was attending a church in Detroit. The young Pastor, Gary Wilkerson, encouraged me and invited me to visit the ministries down in Texas. I went with the church to a seminar in Dallas, Texas, and at the seminar met a man who invited me to speak in his church in Florida. This was the first time I was invited to speak outside of Michigan. About a month later, I headed to Florida with my family. The church I spoke at was small, but I had met a dear couple, Pete and Jane, who invited us to stay with them. These people became close friends, and through the years I've kept in contact with them. Their insight and direction have been a big part of our lives.

While in Florida, doors opened for us. We spoke at a few churches, and even met up with a ministry that would supply the Bible on cassette in different languages so that we could take them overseas. From there we traveled to Texas. We stayed in Lindale, Texas, at the headquarters of World Challenge, YWAM, Calvary Commission, and Last Days Ministry. I enjoyed my stay in Lindale. I was able to meet Leonard Ravenhill, an English evangelist whose writings and teachings had been a challenge to me. I would visit Mr. Ravenhill every time I visited Texas, and we wrote back and forth. His brief letters were like a breath of fresh air. He was a man of prayer and always challenged those who visited him to be the same. On all of his correspondence was this statement: "Is the life you're living worth Jesus dying for?"

One night while in Texas, Gary Wilkerson invited me to go with him to a local radio station. Gary was going to be interviewed. I was just going along for the ride. At the station we met up with the radio hosts, Captain Paul Dilena and his wife, Sonia. I knew Paul's son, Tim, from the fellowship in Detroit; he helped Gary establish the church.

Paul invited us to sit down in front of the radio mikes. I just sat back, and was listening to Paul interview Gary. Then Paul asked Gary to introduce me, and the next thing I knew I was sharing my testimony on the radio. Paul had such an abounding energy and joy that it was contagious. He was able to get me to share things that I thought I had forgotten; things that I thought I would never share.

The program lasted about two hours, and when it was finished, I felt like I had been in a long-distance race. It had all transpired so fast. People called in, wanting to talk with me. Some even wrote us and supported us after that night.

Paul invited me back, and in the future we returned many times. It was not so important to me to be on the radio, but to be around Paul and Sonia. They made us feel like family. Paul called me "a pack-mule for Jesus," and always encouraged me to press on, no matter what anyone thought of me. He truly was an encourager. Of all the people I have seen or met, big-name preachers included, no one was like Paul. He had such an impact on my life. He was a rare jewel in the modern church of our time, and seemed to be able to see what God could do with an individual. He was a joy to be around; as if heaven was right at his feet. He seemed so common, yet so ethereal.

I wrote this book because Paul encouraged me to write my testimony. I never wanted to share the things of my past, but Paul insisted that I should. He has recently gone on to be with the Lord, the One he loved and served so faithfully. I write this book in memory of him; because of him, I had the encouragement to press on. Paul's son, Tim Dilena, pastors a church in the inner city of Detroit. He has also been a good friend, and now walks in the footsteps of his father. Christians need to be encouraged, they need to be challenged, and they need their brother's compassion and strength. I pray that in my life, I, too, can be as Paul Dilena – that my life will have the same impact on others, and that I may be able to encourage people to press on no matter what.

Sharing God's word

Glenn and Frank giving bibles to soldiers

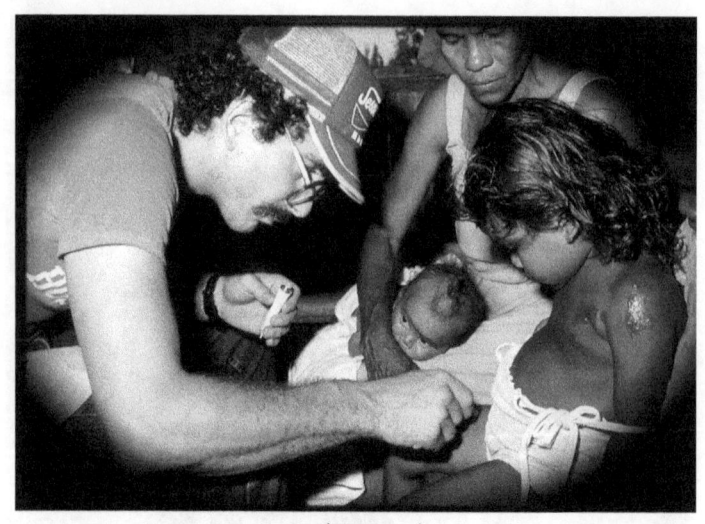

Frank giving aid

Traveling the Mosquito Coast

Chapter 37

Over the years, I did return to Honduras and Nicaragua many times. In Puerto Lempira I was nicknamed "Mosquito Tom." On my third trip, I found out that Wilfrado had been killed. He was shot while on patrol in the jungles. I was thankful that I had been able to bring him the Bibles, and I will always remember the look on his face as though he had asked, "Will you return?" I had returned, and I continue on.

I have been throughout most of Central America, also Cuba, Bosnia, Rwanda, Togo, Sudan, Uganda, Cambodia, Burma, Kosovo, India, and Vietnam. I have had malaria, typhoid, hepatitis, dysentery, and other gifts that come from going to these countries. I've been on leaky boats on rough seas, trying to smuggle Bibles into communist countries; I have been shot at, spit upon, and my life has been threatened by angry mobs. I drove an ambulance into Bosnia during the conflict, with pastors and missionaries traveling in the back of the ambulance, trying to reach the people with the Gospel. I've been on a plane that ran out of fuel, I've been lost in the jungles, and I've walked alone in many strange places.

If someone told me when I first gave my life to Christ that I would be doing such things, I would have thought they were crazy. One of my greatest challenges has been smuggling Bibles into Cambodia through Vietnam in 1990. That particular trip was a trial and test, it proved to me that we as Christians must stay the course, go the distance. The devil will do all he can to get us to turn back. Even using those close to you to bring in doubts and fears. I had traveled there with Tommy Batson who at that time was going through one of the most trying times of his life. However, Tommy taught me what it means that: "Any old bush will do". That it is not the bush that matters but the fire in the bush. God still uses the weak things of the world. The key is to learn to abide, to trust and not draw back. When we headed for Cambodia, arriving at the Houston airport we came across our first obstacle. Because of all the supply we had they would not let us on the plane we were scheduled to depart on.. We were delayed, and the other Christians who were to go with us, left us. The trials did not get easier. When we arrived in Thailand we were told there was no way that we could travel from Thailand to Cambodia with all the supplies we had. The planes traveling at that time, were too small and booked far in advance. Again we met up with our traveling companions in Thailand and again they left us. We found out the only way into Cambodia was to travel by air to Vietnam. I had not expected to go back to the country I fought in however, the mind of man plans his ways, but the Lord directs his steps. What happened on this trip would take up another book, but what pierced my heart with the arrows of God's wondrous power, is that we traveled to Cambodia right through the area I fought in as a soldier. There was a mountain in Vietnam that I was stationed by for awhile, in Tay Ninh province, and this is the mountain we were at the base of when we crossed the border into Cambodia with all the Bibles and supplies. I could not believe I was back with Bibles, fighting another war – the battle for the souls of men. Only the Lord would do such a thing. Take a broken man full of hate and anger, who once carried a weapon to kill, now back in the same place born anew, taking in the Word of God, bringing life instead of death. Once a soldier of this world lost in sin, now a soldier for Christ.

We have four children now. My third child, Anna, we almost lost at birth. She was born with holes in her lungs, and she had to fight for her life. Now she is a young, vibrant individual who seems to always be abounding with energy. My youngest, Jesse, also had problems at birth, but he, too, is a bundle of energy with a soft spirit like his mother. I am thankful for all that God has done, for the family He has given me. We have had some rough times, but God has always seen us through. Truly His grace abounds to the chief of sinners.

Julie and our children - 1995

I have one desire in life, and that is to run the race well, to finish my course. My goal is that I might decrease and that Christ would increase. One soul saved is worth all the difficulties and trials along the way. He saved me, and just as much as He loves me, He loves the street beggar in Bombay, just as much as He died for me, He died for the Muslim terrorist in Afghanistan. He wishes for none to perish. The grace of God in the heart of the Christian is the light that shines brightly to a dark world. We cannot hide this light within our churches. We need to stand and to be seen among those who are perishing. The church was never meant to be a glee club, a place for a bunch of people to come together and make a lot of noise. It is the equipping ground for the saint so that he, too, can be a warrior of light. It is a shame that most people attend a church to hear about someone else who is running the race. We all have a race to run; there is no race in heaven. This is the only life we have to live out the faith within. It is only His grace and mercy that sees us through.

I had worked in India for about eight years. Also many other countries. The greatest gift we can bring is the Gospel. I have seen many men trying to build their own kingdoms in the name of Christ, it is the danger of pride taking over . Those who once started out small, let arrogance take over their hearts. I saw this at home, and abroad, I know it is a danger for my heart as it is for any others. It is Christ alone we must glorify. We must decrease so that He will increase in the lives and souls of men. When we loose sight of this we loose sight of the true gospel.

Africa

Bosnia

Joe & I in Africa

It was a dusty road!

Tommy Batson in Cambodia 1990

Touching one soul for Jesus is worth everything. I have found this fruit of labor in the hearts of Cero and Jenny Meza of Honduras. Cero is a schoolteacher and Jenny, a doctor. They have been a wonderful team that we have had the privilege of working with in Honduras. We organize medical camps in local village churches, often in remote areas. Cero and Jenny work with the sick and needy, along with the team that I bring. We work all day, meeting needs and sharing the Gospel one-on-one with the people. Then at night we invite the villagers out to see the *Jesus* film; after the film, testimonies are shared and those whose hearts are opened to the truth pray to receive Christ. The *Jesus* film has been a good tool for us in many villages around the world. It is the dramatization of the gospel of Luke, translated in over eight hundred languages. The Gospel is the good news, and many are without this wonderful gift of mercy. Touching one soul for Jesus is worth everything.

I would like to write another book just on the mission trips and all that God has done, and the wondrous miracles of seeing souls come into His kingdom. There are so many I could mention that have helped us reach out with the gospel, such as World Missionary Press with all the scripture booklets they have provided us in the last twenty years. Also International Aid, and the many friends that have given of their selves to touch the lives of others. My cousin Joe Faunce who has in the last twelve years, or more has traveled to many countries with me. Joe has given so much of his time resources, and his life, to further the kingdom. He has been such a testimony of the love of God. When our lives are hidden in Christ, we become a flaming torch that those in darkness can be drawn to, and this is how Joe has been to me, and many others in this world.

Each of us that know Him in a real way has the responsibility to share this great love. We are not to be a candle hidden under a bushel. We need to let our lights shine. I know that when we count all things as loss for Christ, we gain all things in Him.

When the love of God fills us, living waters will spill out from us to a lost world, and like those who have gone on before us, we too can be vessels fit for the Master's hand.

To live our lives surrendered to His will is the greatest blessing there is. He loves us – love Him, know Him, and He will use you regardless of where you are. It's not crossing the seas, but seeing the cross – the finished work of Christ and what He has done for and through us, and what He can do for others. We can bloom like a wondrous flower wherever He has placed us – in the factory, at home, in the schools, wherever.

Be willing to let go of all fear, and cast your life into His hands. He will mold you and shape you into the person He has called you to be. He is the potter, and we are the clay. Be pliable, not rigid. If we harden our hearts to His calling, we become useless. However, if we allow His working power within our lives, He will shape us into vessels worthy of His name. His grace and mercy alone accomplishes this.

When the child of God realizes that the Love of God is so deep, so high – that there is no limit; that He is the First and the Last, the Author and finisher of our faith – when we trust we will not have to try to figure out what we need to do, but it will come about just as the seed that grows in good soil. Let God be in control, and all things become possible. It's not about trying to be in ministry; it's about His ministry in us, working out through us. ***Christ in us, the hope of glory!***

I wrote this book to share things that I had not wanted to share; writing about my past is not easy. Some things I have left out, others have been hard to put down on paper. I feel that if one person will respond to Christ through my testimony, then it has been worth it.

If you have read this book and you have never known true freedom, the peace of God, I pray that you will open your heart before Christ. We have all sinned and fallen short of His glory. There is no redemption without His saving grace; there is no other name under heaven by which a man can be saved. Today is the day of Salvation; do not put it off another day. Humble yourself before the living God – He loves you. Today can be the day that you can know true freedom. Your sins can be washed clean, whiter then snow, if you will only believe and receive.

If you are heavy-laden with sin, come to Christ; hold nothing back, surrender your life to Him, and you, too, can be born again. If you truly confess with your mouth and believe in your heart that Jesus is Lord, and have turned from your ways, you will be saved.

Live your life to the fullness God has for you. Trust Him in all things. Let not your heart be troubled, believe and receive. His grace is everlasting, His faithfulness never fails, and His mercy is new every morning. Today is the day of salvation; today is the day for you to surrender your life to Christ and be a soldier for the King! Take the time right now to get on your knees and pray:

"Dear Lord Jesus, I have lived my life my own way. I am a sinner; my heart has been filled with selfishness and pride. Jesus I know that You have died for me. You shed Your blood to wash me clean. I come to You with a humble heart, and I repent of my wicked ways. I ask You, dear Lord, to come into my life, so I may live through You as a child of Your kingdom. This day is the day of my salvation, I am born again, a new creature, old things are now gone, and all things are new. You are the resurrection and the life, and I am Your child, and nothing can ever steal that away.

I love You Lord forevermore, and I look to Your soon return. Amen."

The ministry of Frontline Outreach was established from a burning passion to know Christ. There is no name we desire to exalt other then Jesus Christ our King. God has no big shots, just humble servants called to the Great Commission. He wants to use me, and He wants to use you. Each of us is a precious jewel in His sight; we are living stones being built up, so let us encourage one another to press on to the higher calling of Christ Jesus, to be a soldier for the King!

T. M. Faunce

Jesus did not die for nothing; He died for you!

"But God demonstrates His own love toward us, in that while we were yet sinners, Christ died for us" (Romans 5:8).

"Greater love has no one than this, that one lay down his life for his friends" (John 15:13)

"For God so loved the world, that He gave His only begotten Son, that whoever believes in Him should not perish, but have eternal life. "For God did not send the Son into the world to judge the world, but that the world should be saved through Him. "He who believes in Him is not judged; he who does not believe has been judged already, because he has not believed in the name of the only begotten Son of God. (John 3:16-18).

"But what does it say? "The word is near you, in your mouth and in your heart" that is, the word of faith which we are preaching, that if you confess with your mouth Jesus as Lord, and believe in your heart that God raised Him from the dead, you shall be saved; for with the heart man believes, resulting in righteousness, and with the mouth he confesses, resulting in salvation. For the Scripture says, "Whoever believes in Him will not be disappointed." (Romans 10:8-11).

"Therefore if any man is in Christ, he is a new creature; the old things passed away; behold, new things have come" (2 Corinthians 5:17).

"But God, being rich in mercy, because of His great love with which He loved us, even when we were dead in our transgressions, made us alive together with Christ (by grace you have been saved), and raised us up with Him, and seated us with Him in the heavenly places, in Christ Jesus, in order that in the ages to come He might show the surpassing riches of His grace in kindness toward us in Christ Jesus. For by grace you have been saved through faith; and that not of yourselves, it is the gift of God; not as a result of works, that no one should boast. For we are His workmanship, created in Christ Jesus for good works, which God prepared beforehand, that we should walk in them" (Ephesians 2: 4-10).

"For the word of God is living and active and sharper than any two-edged sword, and piercing as far as the division of soul and spirit, of both joints and marrow, and able to judge the thoughts and intentions of the heart. And there is no creature hidden from His sight, but all things are open and laid bare to the eyes of Him with whom we have to do" (Hebrews 4:12-13).

"If we say that we have no sin, we are deceiving ourselves, and the truth is not in us. If we confess our sins, He is faithful and righteous to forgive us our sins and to cleanse us from all unrighteousness. If we say that we have not sinned, we make Him a liar, and His word is not in us" (1 John 8: 9-10).

"Behold, I stand at the door and knock; if anyone hears My voice and opens the door, I will come in to him, and will dine with him, and he with Me" (Revelations 3:20).

"At the acceptable time I listened to you, behold, now is "the acceptable time," behold, now is "the day of salvation" (2 Corinthians 6:2).

<u>Today, this day you truly can be born again!</u>

Photos that I have taken in the field.

Please, bring me hope!
1 Peter 3:15

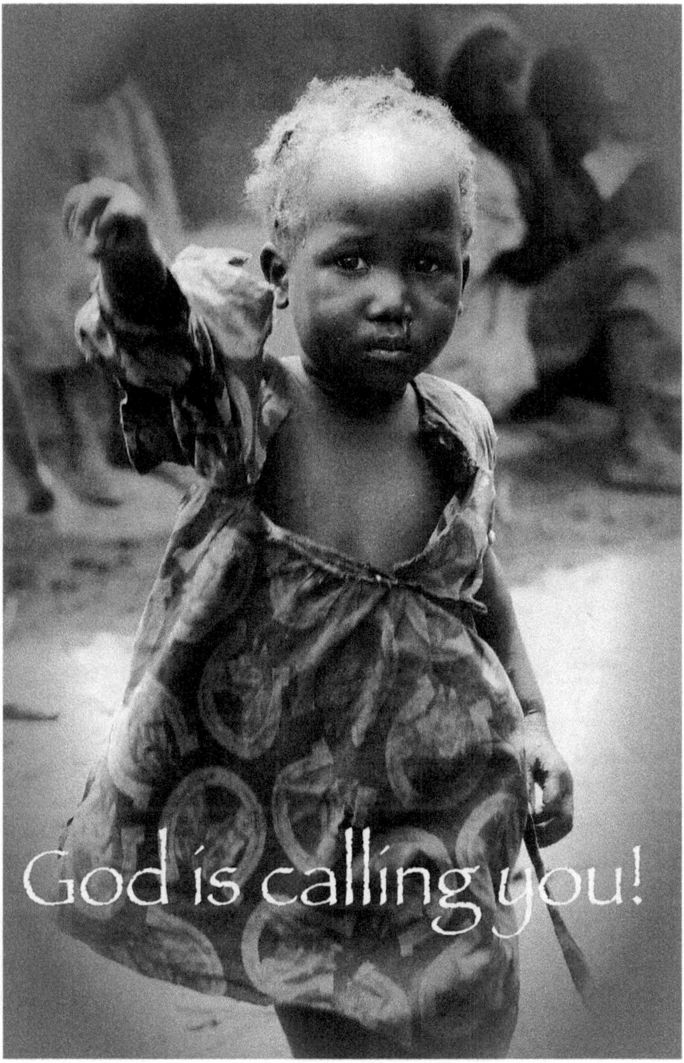
God is calling you!

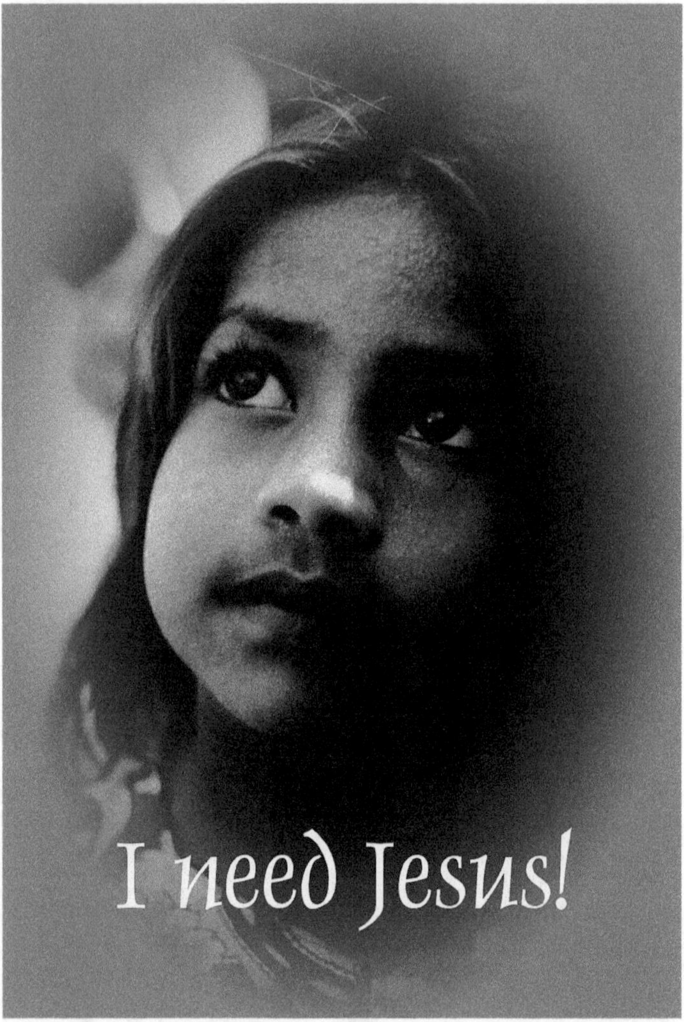
I need Jesus!

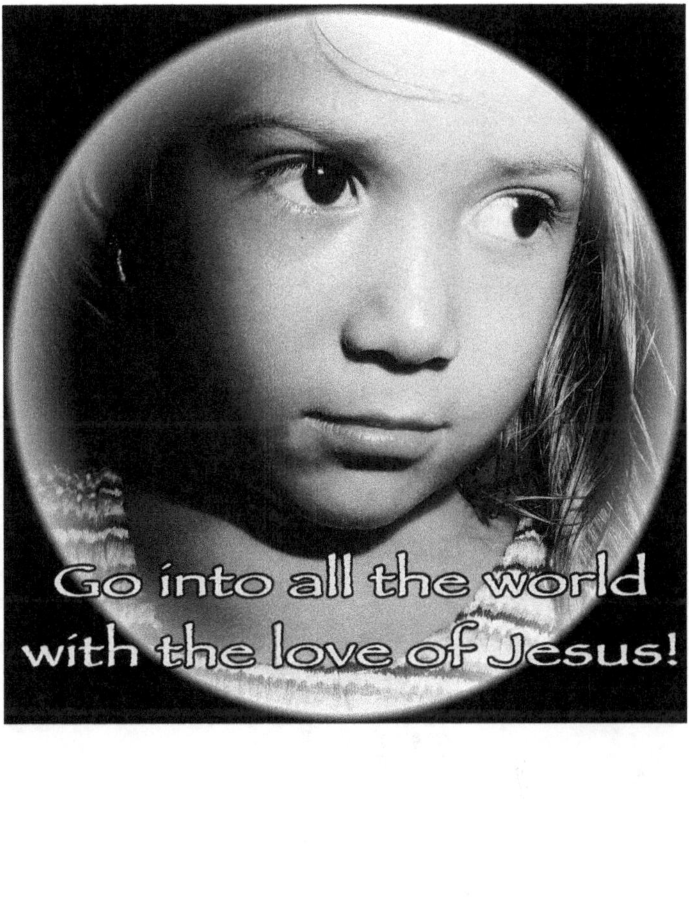
Go into all the world
with the love of Jesus!

Please come soon!

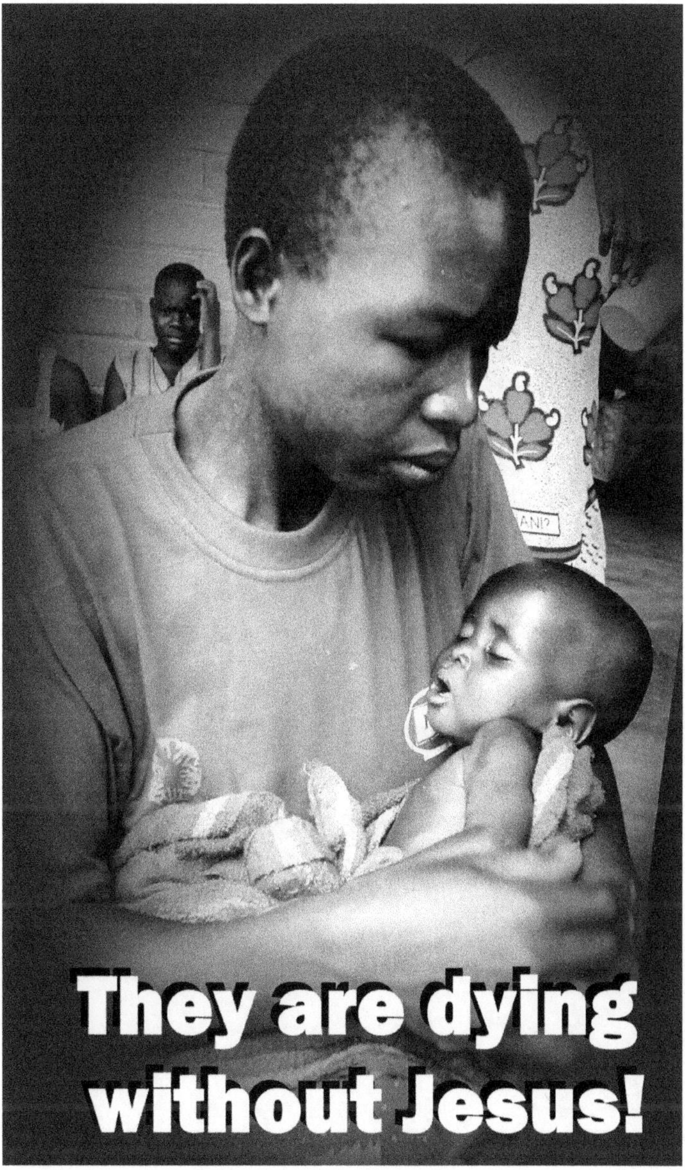
They are dying
without Jesus!

Share my burden!

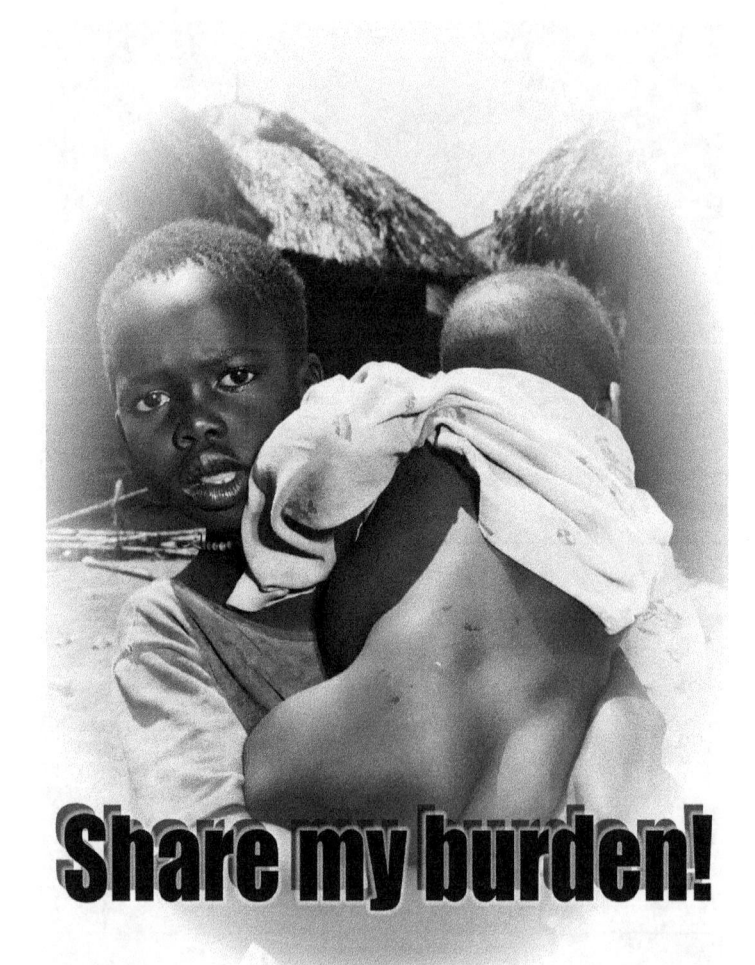

Wipe my tears with His love!

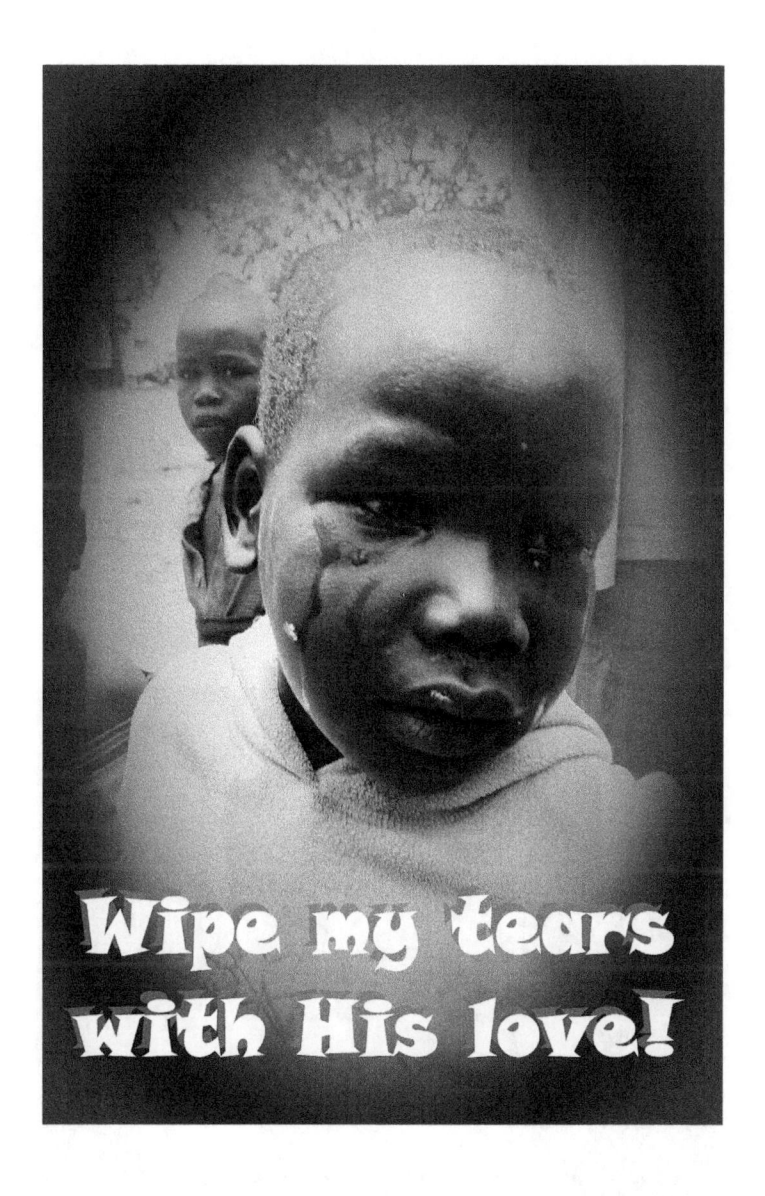

You know we need you!

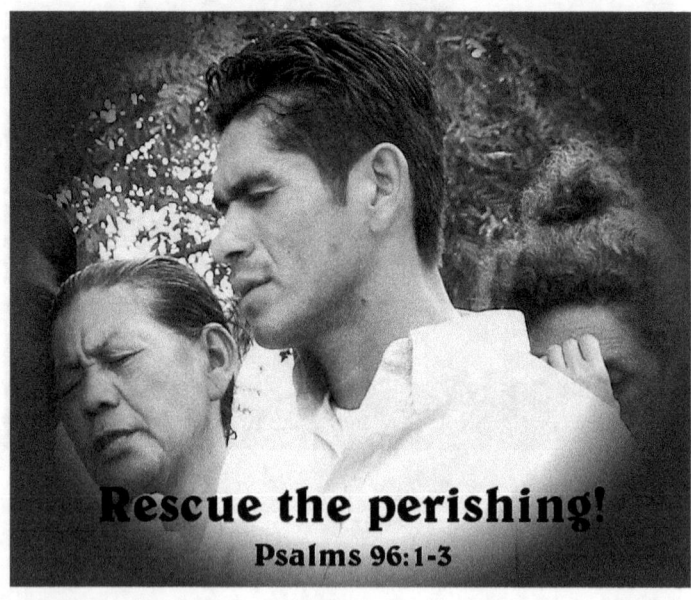

Rescue the perishing!
Psalms 96:1-3

Can you love me?
Romans 15:1

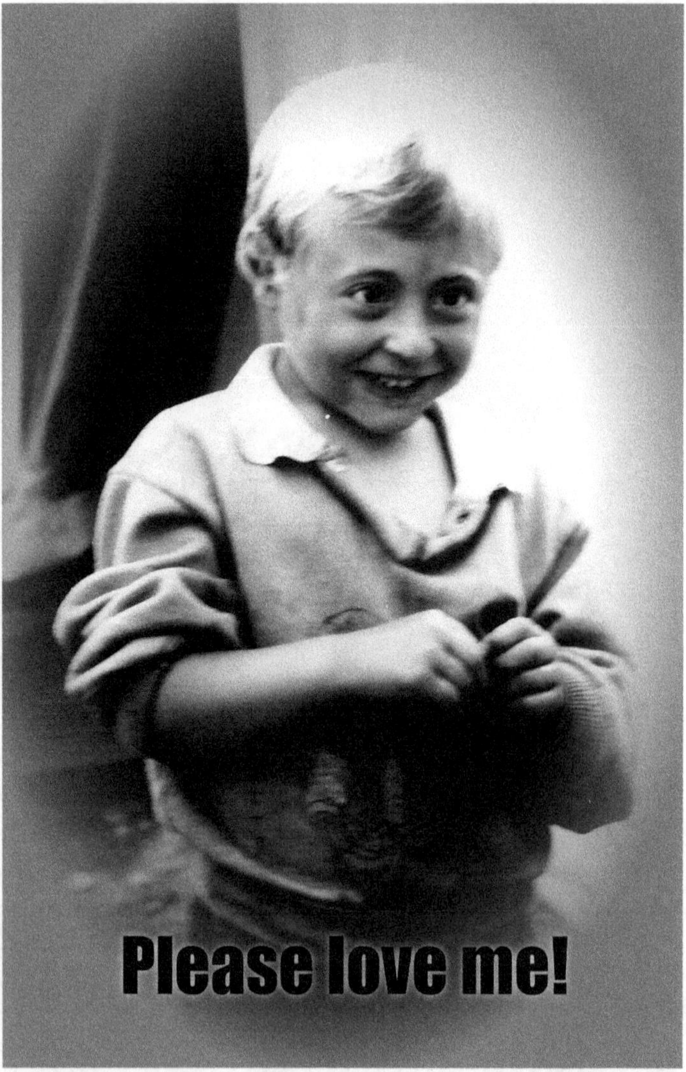
Please love me!

From Defeat to Victory　　　　　　　　　　　　　　　　　　　*T.M. Faunce*

Christ loves us, will you?

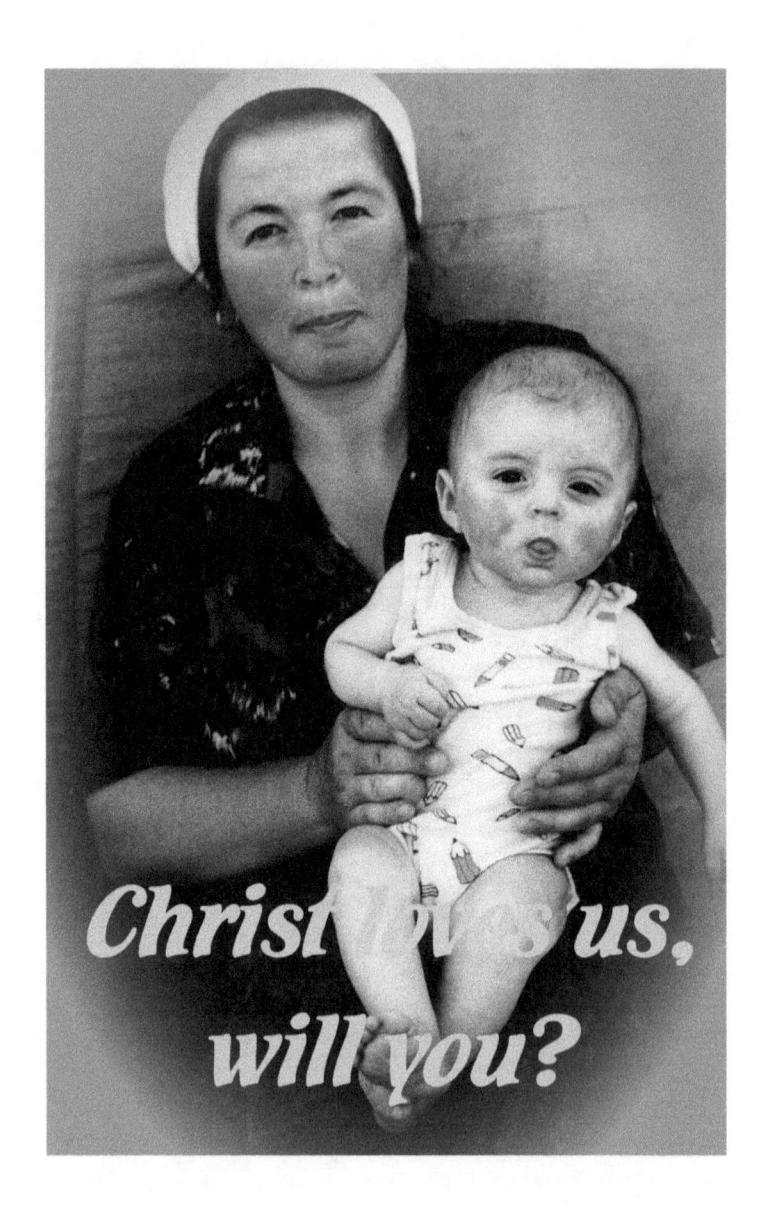

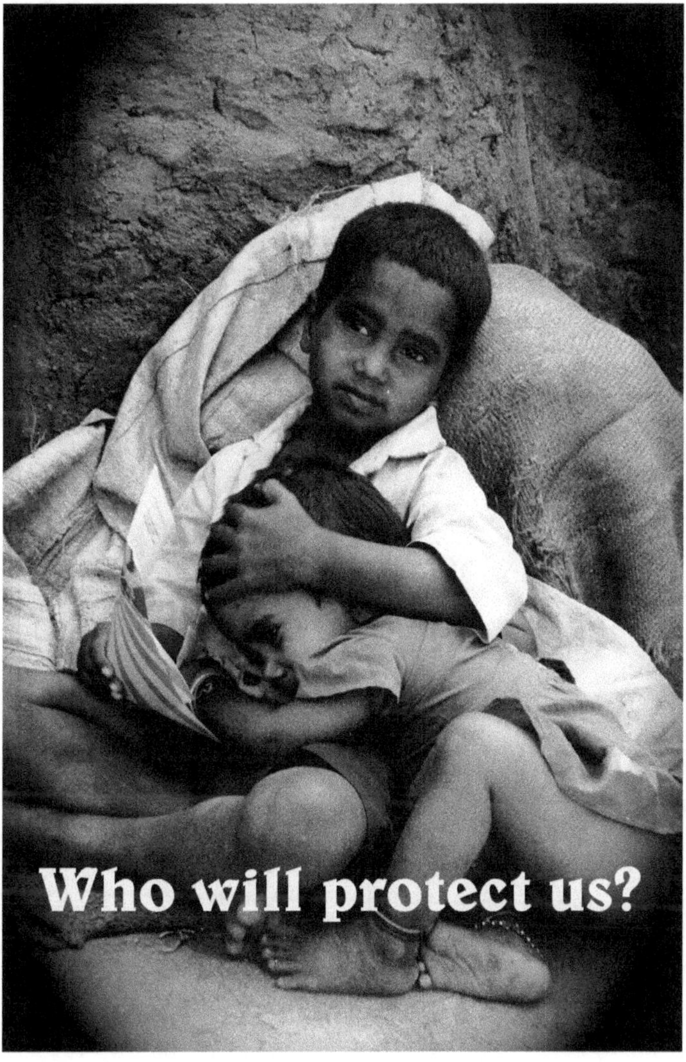
Who will protect us?

From Defeat to Victory *T.M. Faunce*

Do you have room in your heart for me?

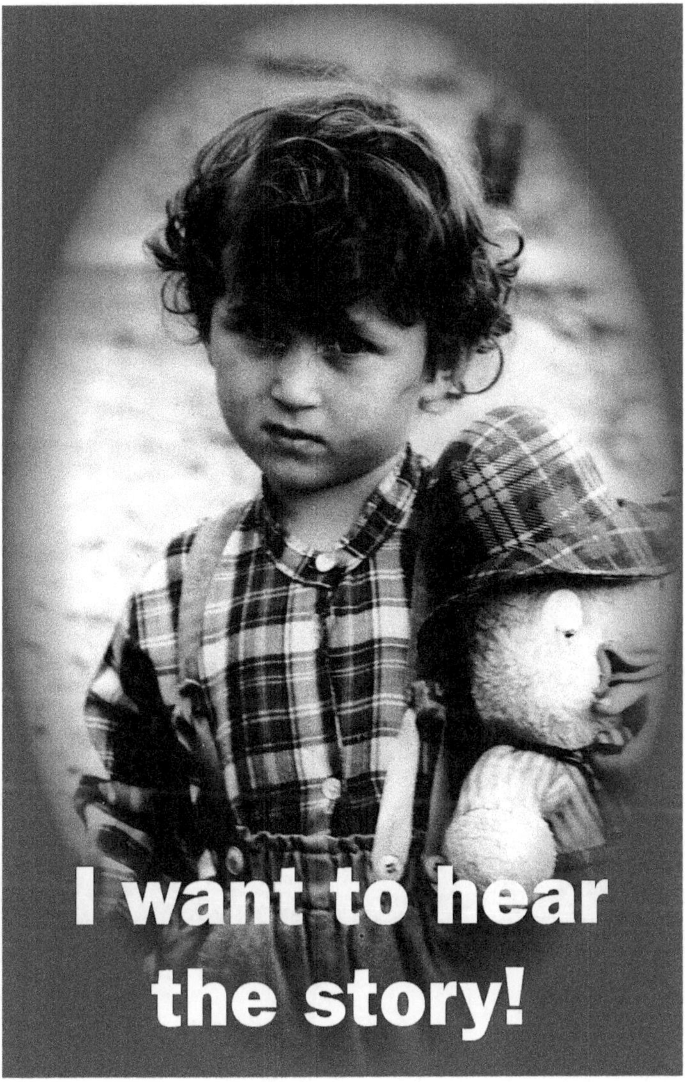
I want to hear
the story!

Jesus Can remove the hate!

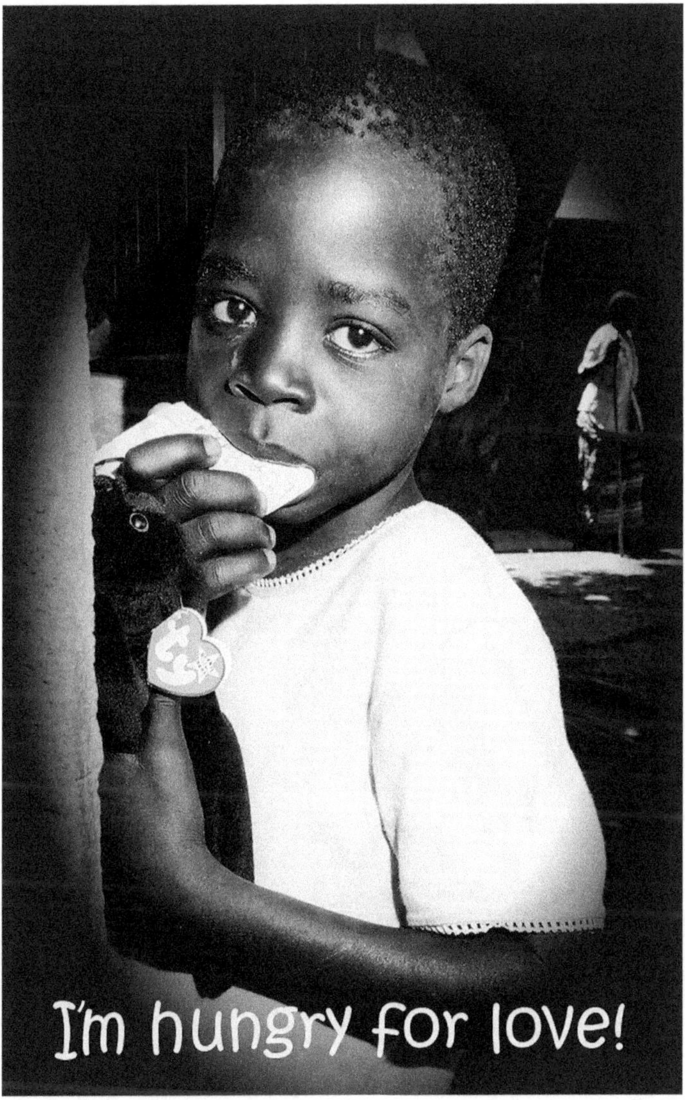
I'm hungry for love!